Rethinking NORMAL

Rethinking NORMAL

A MEMOIR IN TRANSITION

KATIE RAIN HILL

WITH ARIEL SCHRAG

SIMON & SCHUSTER BFYR

NEW YORK   LONDON   TORONTO   SYDNEY   NEW DELHI

SIMON & SCHUSTER BFYR

An imprint of Simon & Schuster Children's Publishing Division
1230 Avenue of the Americas, New York, New York 10020

This work is a memoir. It reflects the author's present recollections of her experiences over a period of years. Certain names, locations, and identifying characteristics have been changed, and certain individuals are composites. Dialogue and events have been recreated from memory and, in some cases, have been compressed to convey the substance of what was said or what occurred.

For information about special discounts for bulk purchases, please contact Simon & Schuster Special Sales at 1-866-506-1949 or business@simonandschuster.com.
The Simon & Schuster Speakers Bureau can bring authors to your live event. For more information or to book an event, contact the Simon & Schuster Speakers Bureau at 1-866-248-3049 or visit our website at www.simonspeakers.com.
Book design by Laurent Linn
The text for this book is set in Arrus.
Manufactured in the United States of America
2 4 6 8 10 9 7 5 3 1
Library of Congress Cataloging-in-Publication Data
Hill, Katie Rain.
Rethinking normal : a memoir in transition / by Katie Rain Hill. — 1st edition.
pages cm
Summary: "In this Young Adult memoir, a transgender girl shares her personal journey of growing up as a boy and then undergoing gender reassignment during her teens" — Provided by publisher.
ISBN 978-1-4814-1823-2 (hardback) — ISBN 978-1-4814-1825-6 (e-book) 1. Hill, Katie Rain—Juvenile literature. 2. Transsexual youth—United States—Biography—Juvenile literature. 3. Transgender youth—United States—Biography—Juvenile literature. 4. Male-to-female transsexuals—United States—Biography—Juvenile literature. 5. Transsexuals—Identity—Juvenile literature. 6. Transgender people—Identity—Juvenile literature. I. Title.
HQ77.8.H55A3 2014
306.76'808350973—dc23
2014013051

FIRST
EDITION

For my wonderful mom

CONTENTS

I HATE FLIES

 I really, *really* hate flies. Is there anything worse than when you're trying to concentrate and some fly is buzzing around your head going, *Bzzz bzzz bzzz*? I mean, yes, there are things that are worse. But right now, sitting here, attempting to begin this memoir, there is nothing I would love more than to have this fly obliterated.

So that's the first fun fact about me: I hate flies. What else?

When this book is published, I'll be twenty years old and a junior at the University of Tulsa.

I lived in five different cities by the time I was twelve, including Okinawa, Japan, and Okay, Oklahoma—population: six hundred twenty.

One of the most romantic nights of my life was making out with a guy until the sun came up while the DVD of *Final Destination*—featuring a gory death every five minutes—played on repeat in the background.

When I was fifteen, I transitioned from being Luke (a boy) to Katie (a girl).

Okay. I just killed the fly. I'm pretty proud of myself, to tell you the truth. It paused on the cafeteria table and didn't see my hand before it was too late. Of course, now that I finally have silence, I've got to get to class. In five minutes I have Philosophy 1003: Socrates to Sartre: Ideas That Shaped Our World. After that I'm meeting up with Todd. I'll tell you more about him later. For now just this one quick detail: Todd gave me a dog tag that's hanging off my backpack that reads, "Property of Katie Motherfucking Hill—Student at PigFarts—Majoring in Being a Bitch." I love it. I love it so much.

1

BLUEBERRY BLUE

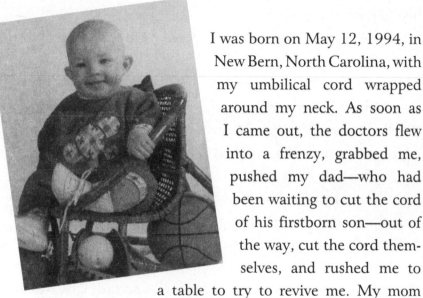

I was born on May 12, 1994, in New Bern, North Carolina, with my umbilical cord wrapped around my neck. As soon as I came out, the doctors flew into a frenzy, grabbed me, pushed my dad—who had been waiting to cut the cord of his firstborn son—out of the way, cut the cord them-selves, and rushed me to a table to try to revive me. My mom caught a glimpse as they whisked me away—my face blue-berry blue from lack of airflow—and she started screaming and crying.

"Where's my baby? Where's my baby?"

She kicked and thrust, trying to get out of the stirrups and out of the bed, while doctors held her down.

I could have died, almost did die. The doctors pinked me back up and brought me to my mom.

"Are you sure he's okay?" my mother asked.

According to my mom, I was completely silent—eerily so for a newborn—fast asleep in her arms. My mom was terri-fied that I'd somehow been damaged from the asphyxiation, that I might be mentally handicapped like her second son from a previous marriage, Josh, was. The doctors reassured her that everything was fine. They brought my dad back in, and he and my mom stared down at me. Soft, full lips. Long eyelashes. And when I slowly opened them, deep blue eyes just like my dad's.

"Look at him," my mom whispered. "He's an angel."

The very first question people ask when there's a baby involved is, "Is it a boy or a girl?" And the instant that question is answered, people begin to place prejudgments and expectations onto that baby. If it's a boy, they imagine the clothes he will be dressed in, what toys he will be given, what sports he will play, the woman he will fall in love with and marry. If it's a girl, they envision party dresses, a bride walking down the aisle, a mom-to-be giving birth herself.

And so it was with me. My parents knew beforehand that they were having a boy, and planned accordingly. After I was born, they wrapped me in my blue-and-white blankie and took me home from the hospital to my blue-painted bedroom. The first couple of years of my life, I barely made a peep. I was the quietest baby you could possibly imagine. I never cried. I never whined. My mom wouldn't even know when to feed me or change my diaper. I would just lie there with that stupid happy baby face, with a diaper full of poop, smiling at everyone. My mom says I was the happiest baby she's ever seen. It was a happiness that would not last long.

WELCOME TO TU!

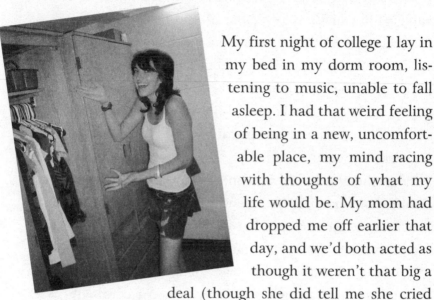

My first night of college I lay in my bed in my dorm room, listening to music, unable to fall asleep. I had that weird feeling of being in a new, uncomfortable place, my mind racing with thoughts of what my life would be. My mom had dropped me off earlier that day, and we'd both acted as though it weren't that big a deal (though she did tell me she cried once she got home). I come from a tough-minded family. We're all emotionally strong but tend to withdraw from one another. We don't like exposing our feelings.

I've always been really independent, which was the result of being chronically depressed from ages seven to fifteen and spending so much time by myself. During those years I would stay locked in my room for days. I've never been afraid to be alone, and I know how to take care of myself. So while I listened to the other students in the hall outside my dorm room all freaking out because they were by themselves for the first time, I thought, *Pshh. I've done this my whole life.* Of course, it never really matters how ready you think you are.

The next morning I woke up early, got dressed in tight blue jeans and a white T-shirt with a British flag design, and took my time doing my makeup. I'd been taking female hormones and living as a girl for about three years. Four months before I'd started college, I'd had GRS (gender reassignment surgery) in which my penis had been turned surgically into a vagina. After years of experiencing shame and hatred of my body, it was an amazing feeling to finally have the right part down there. Not to mention, I could now flirt with guys and know that if something ever happened between us, I wouldn't have to awkwardly explain why I had a penis between my legs.

For some transgender people GRS isn't important. They don't need to change their genitals to be happy. What matters most to them is passing in society as the gender they identify as, regardless of what's in their pants. And for me, even though I did need to have the surgery in order to be comfortable with myself, it was this passing, the way I was finally being seen by others, that mattered the most.

I checked my reflection in the mirror one more time, walked out of the dorms, stepped onto campus, and stared out at the crowds of new people I was going to meet. Three years before, I had been a gangly teenage boy, braces and glasses, face hidden underneath a black hoodie, horrified by the thought of anyone looking at me. I was teased every day, spat on, and called "fag." Now I was Katie, an attractive woman with long, shiny, dark brown hair, high cheekbones, boobs, and a butt that fit into my new feminine clothes perfectly. What can I say? I felt like the queen of the world.

• • •

The first orientation event was a big "Welcome to TU" ice-breaker party. It took place in the school gym, where all the treadmills and elliptical machines had been pushed to the side to make room. The orientation leaders—juniors and seniors—were all pumped up, jumping up and down, whooping and hollering as they led the freshmen, about a hundred of us, onto the basketball court. They formed a human bridge we all had to run through.

"You're part of TU now!"

"Whooo! No turning back!"

Once everyone was inside the gym, we all joined together and did a conga line like a giant snake around the room. It was ridiculously goofy and totally fun. Next they put us into groups of three where one person was supposed to be "the boss" and order the other two to go do absurd things to students they didn't know. In my group were two guys named David and Justin.

"Okay. I'll be the boss," I said. "I want you to . . . go find five people, hug them, and then touch your noses to their shoes."

I know it sounds completely weird, but that was the idea—to break down people's boundaries. It was pretty funny watching David and Justin run off in pursuit of random people to hug.

After that, Justin kept hanging around me. He was a funny, sweet guy, and I suspected he might have a crush on me, because he was acting pretty flirty. I liked him too, but the person I *really* noticed was this tall guy wearing a blue T-shirt and jogging shorts. Damn, was he hot. I couldn't keep my eyes off him.

Our next activity was for everyone to stand in a giant circle while the orientation leaders shouted out statements, and if the statements applied to you, you were supposed to run into the center.

"I'm in a serious relationship and thinking about marriage," a leader shouted out.

I saw the tall guy in the blue T-shirt run to the center, and I felt a pang of disappointment. I also felt a pang of guilt. I was in a relationship too, with my high school boyfriend, Arin, but we'd been having troubles lately. I still loved Arin, though, and started to walk toward the center myself. Then I stopped. *But do I want to* marry *Arin? I don't know.* I started to walk backward, then stepped forward again, then shuffled back. People must have thought I looked crazy.

After the TU party, Justin and I explored the campus together. It felt so good, meeting all these people, making a fresh start in a new environment as Katie, a girl, the person I was meant to be. I wanted to talk to everyone—I was more sociable than I'd ever been in my life.

I spotted a group of students talking outside the cafeteria. One of them was the hot guy from the party.

"Hey, let's go talk with those kids," I said to Justin.

We went over and introduced ourselves. The group was Mark, Jessica, Jon, Liz, and the cute guy, Billy.

"Hey, you're that chick from the party," Billy said to me, grinning. He had the sexiest dimpled smile.

"Yeah, and you're that guy," I said.

I couldn't believe it. It wasn't just that I had noticed *him*. He had actually been checking me out too. I shook my hair nervously and could feel myself blushing. I think everyone could tell there was an instant attraction between us. Despite my crush, though, I was still devoted to Arin and didn't want there to be any confusion.

"I can't wait to tell my boyfriend, Arin, that basically all we've done at college so far is party. He's still in high school," I said.

"Yeah, so is my girlfriend," said Billy.

We all stayed outside the cafeteria, chatting about politics.

"So, who here likes Obama?"

"I think he's doing a good job!"

"What? He's gonna kill us all."

"You're crazy."

We didn't agree on everything, but we were all being friendly and open. I immediately felt comfortable with them.

"Let's take a group photo!" said Liz. She took out her phone and asked a random student walking by to take our picture. We all stood shoulder to shoulder, and Jessica put on an alien mask she was carrying around.

Flash

"Aaah! I look terrible!" said Liz when the guy handed her back her phone.

"You're vain as hell," said Mark, a tall guy with a sassy laugh. He was wearing a T-shirt that said, IF YOU GOT HATERS, YOU MUST BE DOING SOMETHING RIGHT. I told him I liked it.

The group made plans to hang out at one of the campus pools the next day, and to everyone's surprise we all actually showed up. Later on we drove to Target and picked up "college supplies," which consisted of pens, notecards, plastic forks, and forty-pack cases of ramen noodles. Justin bought this giant beanbag that he referred to as his "love sack." We rolled it down the hall into his room, saying, "Justin's sack coming through" and "Watch out; Justin's got a humongous sack" and laughing nonstop.

After that first week we were all pretty inseparable. We'd eat lunch together, walk one another to class, and drive all around Tulsa. Billy and I grew especially close. One day the two of us spent the afternoon hanging out, doing homework in the TU snack shop, and I taught him how to do the cup trick from *Pitch Perfect*. We were taking videos of ourselves, seeing who could do it faster, when Mark and Jessica walked over.

"Aaah! Katie's the master!" said Mark. "Let's see you beat that, Billy."

Billy fumbled his way through the trick, clapping and slapping his cup on the table.

"Oh, that is sad," said Jessica.

"He's actually really good!" I said. "I just taught him twenty minutes ago."

"Thank you, Katie," said Billy, closing his eyes with a modest smile.

"So, what are we doing tonight? Should we go to Majestic?" asked Mark. "I feel like dancing."

"I'm so cracked out from studying. Let's go play *Call of Duty* in your room," said Jessica.

The four of us headed over to Mark and Billy's room, where Billy, Jessica, and I collapsed onto the bed, and Mark fell with a *thump* into Justin's love sack and turned on the video game.

"Why don't we go to the football game tonight?" said

Jessica. "We should show more school spirit. Go, Golden Hurricane!"

"What kind of mascot name is 'Golden Hurricane'?" asked Mark. "That's just weird."

"Where's your TU pride?" said Billy, heading into the bathroom. Two minutes later he opened the bathroom door and flushed the toilet with a flourish.

"Golden Hurricane!" he exclaimed.

We all stared at him for a second and then burst out laughing. From that point on, whenever any of us used the bathroom, we'd flush the toilet and then run out saying, "Golden Hurricane!"

I'd never really had friends like that before, people I could just relax and be myself around. I mean, I'd had friends, but none who'd lived in my immediate vicinity. I'd begun my transition from Luke to Katie my sophomore year of high school and had lost a lot of friends in the process. My junior year, the teasing was so bad, I had to drop out of school and enroll in virtual school, taking all my classes at home online. It was incredibly lonely. The few friends I did have I'd met through queer-teen support groups, but most of them had lived twenty miles away, some farther than that. Now in college I had this tight group of friends, some of whom lived literally down the hall from me. If I had a bad day, I could just call up Billy, and he'd be in my room to talk in less than five minutes. And I was there for him and the rest of them too.

Within the first couple of weeks of school, I started going to TU's Bisexual, Lesbian, Gay, and Transgender Alliance pride events, which took place at the Little Blue House. The

Little Blue House is literally a little blue house on campus that's dedicated to all TU human rights clubs—women's clubs, anti–slave-trafficking clubs, and LGBT groups. The house is minuscule and kind of run-down, but as soon as you walk in, it's warm and homey with a comfy sofa and a long dining table where people can eat a vegetarian lunch every Wednesday. The fridge in the back has a million of those little alphabet letter magnets on it, and each time I'd go, there'd be some new phrase spelled out. "Tulsa A Slut: world's best anagram"—something silly like that.

Every Thursday the Little Blue House hosted an LGBT pride game night, and one time I suggested to the gang that they come with me.

"Pride night? Do you have to be gay to go?" asked Jessica.

"Not at all," I said. "I'm not gay, but I'm a big ally and have done a lot of volunteer work for LGBT stuff. Come on. Game night's fun."

"I got study group," said Billy.

"Sounds cool to me," said Mark. "I'm in."

"Hell yeah, I'm going to game night," said Liz.

"Okay, me too," said Jessica.

Part of me was of course thinking, *Oh God, just tell them you're trans*. But another part of me shut that part down fast. I just wasn't ready. Honestly, I was scared. I had no idea if they would be cool or if they would reject me, and if it were the latter, I didn't want to find out. Some days I imagined just marching up and saying, *"Guess what, guys. I'm trans!"* Other days I lived in terror that they would simply Google me and discover the truth. There'd been an article written about me and my transition in the *Tulsa World* (one of Oklahoma's largest newspapers) my junior year of high school and then a follow-up article done my first week of college, so the information was out there.

When you're close to people, you want to feel like you can share all of yourself, that you shouldn't have to hide just because something about you is different or unexpected. And in a way I felt that my new friends deserved to know. But at the same time this was the start of my new life, and being seen as Katie—just an average girl, no identity politics or medicalized body complications—was part of that. I often fantasized that if it weren't for Google, I could go completely stealth. I could literally get married, come up with some excuse for why I couldn't have kids, and my husband would never have to know about my old life. These friends were a part of that feeling. I didn't want to let that go.

Mark, Liz, and Jessica came with me to pride game night, and we had an amazing time. Our team won a game of Taboo, and we all got to pick out gifts from a bag of trashy prizes. I chose a little kid's medal that was so small, I had to wear it draped over my forehead. Mark picked a sparkly blue hair weave. Afterward we picked up candy and liters of Mountain Dew from the twenty-four-hour campus snack shop and hung out in front of the library, taking videos on our phones.

"Okay, Mark. Model your weave for us," I said.

"I don't like it! It's in my face!" he said, swatting at the thin strays of glittery plastic. "It's everywhere! How do girls do this?"

We were all laughing and acting silly, high off the sugar and the fun of the night.

"Mark! Show us your catwalk!" said Jessica. "Come on, just snap your fingers and walk!"

"No!" Mark said. "I'll look like a faggot— Oops, I can't say that! I just got out of pride!"

I knew he didn't mean to be homophobic, so I gave him a pass.

"Come on, Mark. I've seen you vogue!" I said. We'd all gone dancing at this club called Majestic the previous weekend, and Mark had a pretty fierce vogue. It had actually occurred to me then that he might be gay.

Mark catwalked for a second, then quickly gave up, giggling. "No, I can't do it!"

"You show him how, Jessica!" Liz shouted.

"No! You do it!" she said.

Eventually I just had to step in and show them how it was done.

"It's one foot in front of the other," I said as I catwalked. "Straight line. Straight line. Never touch the hips. Never touch the hips."

"There you go, Katie!" everyone cheered. "Whooo, Katie!"

There's no reason to tell them you're trans, I thought as we all walked back to the dorms. *It's only a small part of who I am. They don't need to know. If they find out eventually, I'll deal with that then.* The easiest thing to do was nothing. And meanwhile I did have someone close to me who not only knew I was transgender but understood it in a way that no one else—or at least very few other people—ever could. Because he, my boyfriend, Arin, was transgender too.

3

THE ARIN JIG

I met Arin my senior year of high school at the Dennis R. Neill Equality Center— or OKEQ—a center in Tulsa that serves the LGBT and allied community. At that point I had been living as a girl for about two years. I was taking hormones to halt any male puberty and to feminize my features, but I hadn't yet had my surgery. Even though I passed as a girl, and had for a while, I still experienced severe bouts of gender dysphoria—anxiety over the way I looked and discomfort with my body, especially my penis.

One random Wednesday night I was feeling especially down. In addition to dealing with my body issues, I was also recovering from a recent, painful breakup with my first-ever boyfriend, Hawthorne. I decided to drop in on a weekly teen trans support group at the center. Talking to and learning from other trans people and giving them advice always made me feel better. The article about me in *Tulsa World* had come out a little less than a year prior, and since then I'd begun giving trans advocacy speeches at high schools and camps and was seen as a role model in the Tulsa queer community.

So I showed up at this meeting, not dressed exquisitely, just jeans and a jacket, no makeup, hair pulled back into a ponytail, and as soon as I walked in, I saw Arin sitting in the group of five or six people. A couple of weeks before that, my mom had been going on and on about this transgender guy she'd seen at the center, and I knew this must be him.

"He is just the most adorable, sexiest trans guy I have ever seen in my entire life," she had said.

"Okay, Mom. I get it. I *just* broke up with Hawthorne and am not exactly ready. Thanks, though."

"No, I don't think you understand. If I were seventeen again, I would totally go after this guy. He is so cute. He is just—"

"Mom, enough!"

As soon as I walked into the meeting at the center, I was like, *Oh my God, that's totally the guy*. Because my mom was right. He was friggin' adorable. He had tousled brown hair and really soft features, and the way he sat, the way his voice sounded when he spoke, warm and kind—he immediately enticed me. Naturally, I sat as far away from him as I could. I introduced myself to the group and told them a little about my story, but was still feeling pretty down and was quiet for most of the meeting.

Afterward Arin came up to me.

"Hey, Katie? It's really cool to meet you. I know who you are."

I had a horrific vision of my mom telling him all about me.

"Um, you do?"

"I read your article in *Tulsa World*," he continued.
Right, of course.
"Oh, cool," I said.
"Cool." He grinned back.

Just then our moms—who were both over in the Parents of Trans Teens meeting that happened at the same time—came back, and Arin and I said good-bye. I got into the car with my mom and started freaking out.

"OH MY GOD, MOM, that boy is SO ATTRACTIVE." She smiled smugly. "I told you so."

A few weeks later I was having another bad night. Sometimes all I could think about was getting surgery. I felt like I couldn't stand having this penis attached to me another second. Why couldn't I have just been born with a vagina? It was Saturday night, so I decided to go to the weekly dance party at Openarms Youth Project—an LGBT-friendly teen community center. I'd like to say I decided to go because, as before, I knew that talking to and helping other trans people would make me feel better. But frankly, that night I just needed people to tell me I looked good. Dances at OYP had been the first place where I'd learned to feel confident about myself. Those dances were the first place where people ever complimented me, people who knew that I was trans and told me I was beautiful. So I put on tight black pants and a low-cut shirt, did my hair, put on makeup, laced up my boots, and went out dancing.

OYP was in full swing by the time I arrived. The ceiling was covered in rainbow streamers, and a glittery disco ball shined strobe lights over throngs of dancing teens. Almost immediately I spotted Arin. *Oh, crap,* I thought, but I needed to play it cool. I veered over to the concessions stand, where I bought a soda and chatted with my friend Adam. Suddenly I heard behind me:

"Oh my God, Katie?"

I turned around and tried to fashion a casual look on my face.

"Oh, hey. You're . . . Arin, right?"

He just stood there, wide-eyed, his mouth hanging open, awkwardly waving at me. He was even cuter than I remembered. He had these really long eyelashes that kind of made him look like he was wearing natural eyeliner. His hair was shaggy, but clean and smooth, and he had on a nice-fitting blue plaid button-down. You could tell he took really good care of himself, kind of metrosexual, in the best possible way. And when I stepped a little closer, he smelled amazing.

I hadn't been to OYP in months, so everyone was excited to see me, and I was soon swept up in another conversation. A little while later I was outside talking to my friend Allen when Arin came up again. *Okay, Katie,* I told myself, *relax. Just strike up a friendship with this guy.* Arin and I started chatting about our childhoods and a little bit about our transitions.

The DJ put on Bruno Mars's "Grenade," and I felt compelled to dance. I went inside while Arin and Allen stayed talking.

As I danced, I caught a glimpse of Arin. He was watching me with this giant smile. I know it seems obvious in retrospect that he liked me, but at the time all I could think was, *Oh God. He's laughing at me because he thinks I look stupid dancing. I thought I was a good dancer, but I guess not? Just keep dancing. Don't worry about it.*

Arin's friend Dale grabbed him and pulled him onto the dance floor. As soon as Arin started dancing, I stopped worrying about my dancing being bad. He was terrible! I mean really, the boy couldn't dance worth crap. But it was pretty adorable. He'd do a little hop, then stick his arms close to him, then wiggle his butt. He basically looked like he was jumping and wagging his tail. So as he was doing his little Arin jig, he was staring and grinning at me, and I started smiling back, now feeling like a pretty exquisite dancer, getting wild and all over the place. Then everyone started dirty dancing, and Arin and I were really going at it, making faces at each other and laughing. Eventually it got too hot and sweaty, so I went outside to cool down. Arin came too.

"So, hey," he said. "I was wondering if I could get your number?"

I wasn't sure whether he liked me or just wanted my number to get advice on transitioning, but I entered it into his phone. When we'd chatted earlier, I'd found out he was only a few months into his, hadn't even started taking T (testosterone) yet. I told him I bet I could predict exactly how his transition would go.

"Within a day of your first T shot, your voice will crack," I said.

"Really?"

"Within the first month and a half, you'll start growing hair." I examined his facial features. "It will grow here, here, and here," I said, pointing to his upper lip, his jawline, and where his sideburns would be. "You'll also get a happy trail here," and I touched just below his belly button. He blushed. "It will be a single line going from the top of your torso all the way down. A few months later the hair will fill out over your stomach. I bet you that's exactly how it goes."

"Okay," he said with a challenge in his voice. "We'll see if you're right."

(FYI, I was. To this day I predicted his transition to a T. Ha-ha, no pun intended.)

My friend Beth invited me to sleep over after the dance, and as soon as we got to her house, I Facebook messaged Arin, telling him I'd had a really good time chatting. The next morning he still hadn't written back.

"Beth! He's not writing or texting me. He doesn't like me." I collapsed facedown on Beth's bed.

"Calm down," she said. "Don't you know the two-day rule? He has to wait two days."

"I don't like that game-playing crap," I said, sitting up. "He needs to stop playing games and frickin' text me."

Later that morning, after I'd gone home, my patience was rewarded—he *finally* texted.

Hey Katie it was great meeting you. You're really pretty.

I immediately called Beth.

"Aaah! Beth! He wrote back!" I said.

"Couldn't even wait two days . . . ," said Beth.

I hung up with Beth and texted Arin back, asking what he was up to that day.

Going to a movie, he responded.

I stared at my phone, waiting to see if he was going to invite me. After doing this for a minute that felt like an hour, I just texted back.

Cool. I haven't seen a movie in a long time. I'd like to see a movie.

Cool. You should.

Good Lord! Did this boy want to date me or not? I continued texting him hints to invite me, but that apparently wasn't happening. Instead I went to Petco with Beth to help her select a pet turtle, and then we rode bikes around the River Walk. I kept texting with Arin the whole time, and when he was on his way to the movie, I just broke down and invited myself.

I might have some free time. I could join you.

Sure!

The movie was *The Cabin in the Woods*. I arrived a little late, after it had started, and spotted Arin sitting toward the front in a pink T-shirt. I slipped into the seat next to him, and he smiled at me through the dark with his cute little baby face. I then spent the entire movie trying to give him cues to hold my hand or put his arm around me. It was kind of ridiculous how blatantly obvious I was, rubbing up against him, yawning, acting like I was cold. But he wouldn't do it. He just sat there, as stiff as a stone. He seemed kind of traumatized, actually. When the movie was over and we walked out, I realized *his mom and little brother had been sitting two rows behind us the entire time*.

"That was a fun movie! Oh, I'm Denise," Arin's mom said, extending her hand.

"Uh, hi. I'm Katie," I said.

"Oh my God, you're so hot!" said Arin's eleven-year-old brother, Wesley, staring at me. That was profoundly awkward.

Thank God we hadn't actually done anything!

. . .

After that first (if you could call it a) date, Arin and I went out a few more times. We got lunch, went to the movies again, but still hadn't kissed. I desperately wanted us to make out, but it was also just great to have someone I could talk to who understood my issues around being trans. It was almost like he became my instant best friend—my best friend I was totally attracted to and infatuated with. One day after we went out for pizza, I dropped him off at his family's business, Danco Pump and Supply. We got out of the car by a large warehouse, hugged good-bye, and then looked into each other's eyes for this intense moment. I tried to send him a telepathic message: *Kiss me.* But still nothing, so then I did my classic Katie move of play-pushing him and walking away, giving a flirty glance over my shoulder. He gave me this deer-in-the-headlights look, and I knew he was thinking the same thing I was. We needed to kiss already!

Our next plan to see each other was at the Equality Gala. Every spring OKEQ throws a gala event, and that year I was receiving the Carolyn Wagner Youth Leadership Award for work I'd done in the community. I had to give a speech and was pretty nervous. The Equality Gala is a huge deal in Tulsa. It's held at the Tulsa Convention Center ballroom, and there would be more than six hundred people. Ticket prices ranged from $150 up to $20,000 for a premium table for ten. I was able to bring my whole family—my mom; dad; twelve-year-old brother, Jake; and twenty-one-year-old half brother, Derik—and give Arin and his family free tickets as well. I bought a slim black evening gown, and my mom took me to get my hair done the day of.

When I first walked into the convention center hallway, there was a table with giant cartoon portraits of the four people receiving awards. Jake pointed and laughed at mine, but I loved it. A band was playing in the convention center, and drag queens in elaborate, sparkly costumes with five-inch heels ran around entertaining everyone for the pre-party until it was time to head into the ballroom.

Through the crowd of tuxes and fancy dresses, I spotted Arin. He was wearing a crisp suit with a striped tie and looked painfully handsome. As soon as he saw me, he walked right up.

"You look beautiful," he said, and handed me a single rose in coral wrapping. I'd mentioned *once* that I preferred single flowers to bouquets, and he'd remembered.

"You look great too," I said, staring into his eyes. God, I wanted to kiss him so bad.

"Congratulations, Katie!" said Toby Jenkins, the director of OKEQ, coming over and giving me a hug. "I can't wait to see you up on that stage."

My heart started beating nervously again. Soon the drag queens were ushering everyone into the ballroom, and as I walked in, I almost gasped. I'd never been to anything like this before. Wavy rainbow lights danced all across the ceiling, in and out of hundreds of rainbow balloons. There were dozens of dining tables spread with fancy white tablecloths and scattered with colorful confetti. The floor was covered by a gorgeous maroon carpet with swirling white designs, and in the center of the room was a shiny hardwood dance floor. At the front, black stairs led to a giant stage. The one I would soon be walking up onto.

My family and I sat down at our reserved table toward the back. They all gorged on the stuffed roast chicken, ratatouille, and Waldorf salad, but I was too nervous to eat. Arin was seated with his family a few tables over, and we kept glancing over at each other and sharing these loaded, romantic grins. I felt my body tingle with anticipation as I thought, *Cross me off the singles list right now. I'm taken.*

"What are you going to say for your speech?" my mom asked.

"It's fine. I got it covered," I said in a blasé tone—a lie. I had no idea. I looked anxiously down at my rose from Arin and tried to formulate what I was going to say. I'd done public speaking before at high schools and camps, but never to this many people.

Everyone quieted down as Toby Jenkins came onstage dressed in a superhero costume. He started running around making "whooshing" noises.

"I'm Gay Man, come to save the day!" he exclaimed. He then read the results of the auction that had taken place during the pre-party. It was incredible—people had bid as much as two thousand dollars on a bouquet of flowers, all to help the Equality Center. Toby then announced a few other award recipients, and they each got up onstage and thanked people. I admired them all greatly, and listened and applauded while at the same time nervously going over and over my own speech in my head.

"And now I'd like to introduce someone very dear to me, the recipient of the 2012 Carolyn Wagner Youth Leadership Award . . ."

My heart started pounding furiously.

"Miss Katie Rain Hill!"

The room exploded in applause as I stood up, my entire body shaking, my hands clammy with sweat.

"I'm not missing this," said my mom, getting up too. "We're coming with you to the front." So my whole family walked with me to the front of the room, and then I climbed the stairs up onto the stage. Despite everything I'd planned to say, as soon as I got up there and looked out at all the hundreds of faces, my mind went completely blank.

"Hello," I began, my voice wavering. "I had a whole speech planned out, but honestly, I can't remember what it was."

Everyone laughed, and I began to find my strength. "So I'm just going to speak from my heart. I've come a long way in the past couple of years, and we've come a long way as a community."

I talked about courage, the courage it can take to just be yourself, and the courage to do whatever you can to help others.

"I promise I will make you all proud," I said. "I promise I will do what I can to make this world a better place. I can't thank you enough for what you've done for me."

I realized that a lot of people were crying.

"Thank you," I said again, and walked off the stage as the whole room rose to their feet, applauding.

"She's one of my heroes, and I want to send this one out to Katie Rain Hill, whom I love!" the singer of the band said into the mic, and then they launched into "You Are So Beautiful." Everyone hit the dance floor.

The last song of the evening was a slow dance that Arin and I shared.

Our moms had previously agreed that Arin could spend the night. When the dance was over, we climbed into the blue Hummer my brother Derik had borrowed to drive us around and headed home. Arin and I sat in the backseat, my head resting on his shoulder.

While Arin relaxed in the family room, I was changing into my pajamas in the bathroom, and I dropped my award—this big, heavy obelisk—right onto my toe. My foot started bleeding all over the place. But I figured, *That's okay. Arin should probably witness my extreme clumsiness sooner rather than later.*

"Don't mind me," I said, coming into the living room in my pink flannel pajamas holding a bloody towel around my foot.

"Oh my God, are you okay?" he asked.

"Oh, Katie, not again," my mom said, passing through the room.

Arin helped me clean up my foot and put a bandage around it. He then changed into his pajamas, and I laid a pallet of blankets on the floor. We put on *Final Destination*, and to this day I cannot tell you a single thing that happens in that movie. We spent the whole night talking while the DVD played over and over. When we were finally ready to fall asleep, I cuddled up next to him and he cuddled up next to me, and then we looked at each other really awkwardly for maybe a full minute. And I'm thinking, *All right. If he's not going to make the first move, then I'm going to.* So I leaned in and kissed him. It was long and passionate. It was beautiful. It was probably the best first kiss I've ever had—apart from the fact that in the background someone in *Final Destination* was screaming, "AHHHHHH! MY ARM JUST GOT RIPPED OFF" or something like that. Meanwhile, we kept kissing, whispering,

"You're so handsome. . . ."

"You're so beautiful. . . ."

After a while of making out, Arin asked, "Will you be my girlfriend?"

"Yes," I whispered, and I wrapped my arms around him and laid my lips on his.

We finally fell asleep at around five a.m. but had to wake up a few hours later. Jake was going over to his friend Lane's house to ride motocross bikes, so Arin and I decided to go with him. While Jake and his friend rode the track, Arin and I walked around the surrounding woods together, just talking and making out. It was our first day as boyfriend and girlfriend, and we were both giddy and loopy from having barely slept.

"I can't believe I'm finally dating you!" he said.

"Tell me what you thought the first moment you saw me," I said.

"I thought you were drop-dead gorgeous, duh. What did you think of me?"

"Too cute for words."

"So you're *sure* you want to date me?"

"Yes! Are you sure *you* want to date *me*? You're not just doing it out of pity? Because I've had that happen."

Being trans, we still each had a certain amount of inse-curity. We were so used to feeling alienated from our bodies and being looked at as freaks. Part of us still couldn't believe that someone actually liked us—that it wouldn't turn out to be some cruel joke.

"Are you kidding?" said Arin. "I mean, I get it, 'cause people have dated me out of pity too. But that is *not* what this is. I'm head over heels for you."

I felt my face flush. "What's the most interesting thing about me?" I asked.

"Your mystery," said Arin. "The things I don't know and can't wait to find out." Then he took my hands, pushed me softly against a tree, and kissed me. It was the perfect romantic day.

We had no idea that six months later a media frenzy would blow up all around us.

"OH MY GOD, THERE'S A TRANSGENDER PERSON AT OUR SCHOOL"

I never did tell Mark, Jessica, Jon, Liz, and Billy that I was trans, but I'm pretty sure they found out on their own. In October of my first year at college, *Inside Edition* contacted me. They had read my follow-up interview in *Tulsa World* in which I talked about Arin, and they wanted the two of us to do a TV segment on transgenderism. The *Inside Edition* episode aired later that month. Arin and I watched as our faces flashed onto the TV with the title card "The Perfect Match" in pink letters and a design involving arrows. The producers showed clips of Arin riding his dirt bike and lifting weights, photos of me at the hospital after surgery, photos of Arin in a pageant dress as a girl, and video of us in our bathing suits hanging out by the pool. A man's voice-over proclaimed, "The two teens couldn't be happier together. Looking at them today, you would never know that she was once a boy and he was once a she."

It was thrilling to watch myself on TV, but I also wondered nervously if any of my new college friends might see it. *Nah, they're not watching* Inside Edition, *I told myself. They barely watch any TV, and if they do, they just want to veg out to* SpongeBob SquarePants.

Meanwhile, despite being portrayed by the media as a perfect couple, Arin and I were having increasing relationship problems. Arin couldn't grasp what it was like for me to be in college with a full-time study load—he wanted everything to stay the same as it had been that summer. He would get upset if I didn't drive the forty-five minutes to Broken Arrow to spend the night at his house, just to wake up at six thirty a.m. and drive forty-five minutes back to school. I loved Arin, I didn't want to break up, but I could feel myself slowly pulling away. And I found myself thinking about Billy more often than I should have been.

One day I was eating lunch with Billy in the cafeteria and confessed how I was confused about Arin.

"Why don't you just break up with him?" Billy asked, chomping into a burger.

"Come on. You know it's not that easy," I said. "Arin's the most important person in the world to me . . . and I can't stand the idea of hurting him."

"What if staying with him is hurting him more?" asked Billy.

I thought about that one for a moment.

"All I know," Billy continued, "is that you're a ten. Ten body. Ten face. Ten personality. You could have anyone."

I blushed. "You're a ten too," I said.

Just then Jessica came up to our table.

"Hey, Jessica. What's up?" I said.

Jessica gave me this weird, intense stare, then looked over at Billy.

"I talked to this football player the other day, and he said there's a transgender person who goes to our school."

Oh shit. Oh no, I thought. *Just play it cool.*

"What?" I asked. "What are they talking about? Who said that? What's going on?" And by "play it cool," I mean I totally started rambling.

"I don't even know what that is," said Billy.

Jessica shot me one last look and then flounced off.

"Jessica's a weirdo," said Billy.

"Yeah," I said, poking at my disgusting cafeteria spaghetti.

Did Jessica know? Had that football guy seen *Inside Edition*? Had Jessica Googled me? Billy kept talking, but my mind was swimming. Being in the media was important to me; I wanted to educate people about trans issues, and I wanted to be there for other trans people who were struggling with coming out. But I also just wanted the normal life I was finally getting to live. I'd spent my whole life as Luke, a boy—someone I wasn't—and now I just wanted to grab what teenage years I had left. Deep down I knew my college friends would find out eventually, but I guess I just kept hoping that it wouldn't have to be on that day.

Jessica never mentioned the transgender thing again, and a week later we all went out dancing at Majestic. We had a great time dancing to eighties hits, watching Mark vogue (if that boy isn't gay, he should at least consider getting into drag—he's got serious talent!), and topping the night off with burgers and chocolate shakes at Sonic. Billy had to go to a park a half hour away for a geology lab the next morning. Since I had a car, I offered to drive him. And because we'd have to wake up super-early, I suggested he just spend the night in my room.

"I mean, you can go back to your room, but I don't want to be waiting on your ass when your alarm doesn't go off in the morning," I said.

"Ha, cool," said Billy. "I guess I'll just crash at yours. I can sleep on the floor."

All of us had crashed in one another's dorm rooms at some point, so it didn't feel that out of the ordinary. When we got back to my room, though, it was really cold, and I realized I didn't even have any extra blankets.

"You should just sleep in my bed," I said.

I know this seems like I was trying to seduce him or something, but I honestly saw the whole thing as totally innocent and really just for convenience.

So we got into our pajamas, turned out the lights, and got into bed. And that was when it hit me. *Oh my God, I'm in cuddling distance of Billy. This is* not *good.* I quickly turned around to face the wall. *Just go to sleep,* I told myself. *Just shut your brain off. Do not do anything. You love Arin. It's not worth it.*

"Good night, Katie. I had fun today," he said.

"Me too," I said.

Then Billy rolled over and put his arm around me. I can't lie—it felt amazing. I absolutely love being held as I fall asleep. Arin would hold me when the lights first went out, but then he'd get uncomfortable and roll over to the other side of the bed. We always slept with all this space between us. But now I had Billy, my crush, pressed up close to me, his strong arm around me. *Oh, Billy . . . ,* I thought.

We didn't kiss, but we did spend the whole night cuddling in a not-exactly-just-friends way.

The next day both Billy and I pretended like nothing had happened. I drove him to his geology lab, and we spent the whole trip talking in short, awkward sentences. The drive back was a little more relaxed; we were able to goof around and joke a bit, but I noticed he was looking at me in a different way. There was a new kind of glow behind his eyes. It made me excited, but it also gave me an ominous feeling. Somehow I knew I was going to get hurt.

A couple of weeks later everyone in the group stopped talking to me. They'd go out with one another but not invite me, and whenever I asked one of them if they wanted to hang out, it was always, "Oh . . . I'm too busy." And two hours later I'd see a picture of the person on Facebook with the rest of the gang at some frat party. I thought maybe Billy felt weird about our night together, but what was with the rest of them? Did Jessica actually know I was trans? Had she told them? I decided to just call her.

"Hey, Jessica. Want to have dinner tonight? I'll pay."

"Oh, hey, Katie. Um, sorry. I have a lot of homework tonight. I'm gonna stay in."

Next I tried Mark.

"Mark! What are you up to? Let's go to Sonic."

"I am deep into *Call of Duty* right now. I'm not going anywhere."

What the hell was going on? Frustrated and confused, I tried Jessica again.

"Jessica, come on. You can take a break to get dinner, right?"

"I told you, I have plans with my friend Tara."

"I thought you had homework."

"Right, whatever."

We hung up.

Maybe they just thought I was boring. But probably, whether through *Inside Edition* or Google or rumors, they'd found out I was trans. I still don't know for sure why they abruptly cut me out. While I tell myself that I don't care, that I don't want to be friends with people like that anyway, the truth is, it broke my heart. I was finally the girl I'd waited so long to be, and I'd had this whole group of awesome, fun, smart people who'd seen me and liked me for who I was. Not as Luke, not as Katie the transgender girl, but as just Katie. And then they were gone.

As I fell into loneliness and depression after the loss of the group, I began to recall the dark years of my childhood, the suicidal years I had been trying to forget. For me those began as early as seven.

5

For the first five years of my life, my dad and I were as thick as thieves. We all lived on a military base in Okinawa, Japan, in a little white house with a squat palm tree out front, and as soon as my dad would get home from work, he'd scoop me up and we'd spend the entire evening playing together. We'd look through airplane books (my toddler-age obsession) on the living room carpet, or he'd take me out to his car, sit me on his lap, and let me play with the steering wheel. He'd waited until late in life to have children—he'd divorced his first wife when she'd told him she had decided she didn't want kids—and had me when he was forty. I was his firstborn son and felt wholly and unconditionally loved. He was Major Randy Hill, United States Marine Corps, strong and muscled, with thinning light blond hair and twinkling kind eyes. I worshipped him.

In the evenings after preschool my mom would cook dinner, and I'd sit around the house, just waiting for Dad to come home. I remember one time when I was four, I was playing in my sleeping bag in the hallway when he finally walked through the door.

"What's this in the hallway?" he said. "It looks like a bag of trash! I better go take this out."

"No! Daddy! Stop," I said, giggling as he picked up the sleeping bag with me inside.

He took me out to the garbage can, opened the lid, and put me in.

"Daddy!" I said, poking my head out.

"Oh my God!" he said, feigning utter shock. "There's a kid in there! I better take this back inside."

My mom was the aquatics director of the swimming pools on the base, and every weekend my dad would take me and give me swimming lessons. I was nervous the first few times I got into the water, and wound up swallowing way too much water, but when I was with my dad, I felt like I could do anything.

"That's it, Luke. You got it. Just lift your head up and keep on moving those arms and legs. That's a feisty kick you got!"

For those few years he was the best dad any child could want. But I would not turn out to be the son he thought I was.

When you're a toddler, you don't think about gender or sex. They aren't even concepts you fully understand. But from around the age of two, I knew that something with my body was off. I couldn't explain why, but I was certain that my penis was not supposed to be there. I would see my mom get out of the bath. I'd notice her vagina and think, *Well, maybe mine will grow into that when I'm older.* I remember going to her, tugging on my genitals, and saying, "Mom, I want this off." She didn't think too much of it, just a little boy bothered by the protrusion of his penis. But for me it was more than discomfort. It was a profound alienation from my body that I had no idea how to articulate.

I would often fixate on older girls. There were twin sisters who lived down the street from us who would babysit me along with their six-year-old sister. All three sisters were tall, blond, leggy girls with scrunched-up faces who liked to wear pink skirts and tank tops. We would often play house, and even though I was four, I was always "the baby." They would swaddle me up in a towel for diapers and pretend to feed me.

"Is baby Luke hungry? Does he need another bottle? Elizabeth, go warm the milk!"

"You warm the milk! I'm singing baby Luke a lullaby."

I remember loving their attention. I had this Mrs. Potato Head toy and would ask the twins to help me clip her clunky yellow earrings over my own ears. Pretty soon I never wanted to take those earrings off. I'd prance around the house with my earrings and a scarf or my blankie draped over my head to resemble long hair.

"That child has always got to have something hanging off his head," my mom would say.

I'd often beg to be allowed to wear a dress to day care.

"You're a little boy, sweetie," Mom would say. "Boys don't wear dresses."

"Why?"

"That's just the way it is."

"But don't you think I'd look pretty in a dress? I want to look pretty, like you."

"Oh, Luke, you're just being silly."

While this confusion began to stir inside me, my dad was having increasing problems of his own. Before I was born, he had been the commanding officer of the Alfred P. Murrah Federal Building in Oklahoma City, the building that Timothy McVeigh blew up on April 19, 1995. We were living in Japan when it happened, and my dad lost a number of friends and people who had worked under him. As my mom told me, the guilt of not being there, not being able to somehow stop it or help, tortured him, and he soon turned to drinking. I didn't know it at the time, but according to my mom, my dad began drinking when I was just a few years old. But his troubles started long before that.

The story of my dad's childhood in rural Idaho is harrowing. His mother committed suicide when he was eight years old, shot herself in the head, and my dad was the one who found her. His father had a drinking problem, and after his wife's suicide, he would take off on drinking binges, leaving the four kids—Larry; my dad, Randy; Leslie; and Shauna—alone for months. They survived by eating what scraps they could find around the house. Shauna was still in diapers and developed a severe infection from the diaper never being changed, causing her to scream in pain until someone heard and called child welfare. The kids were split up. Randy and Larry were sent to the grandparents, while the sisters went to an aunt and uncle, both families devout Mormons. As soon as Dad turned eighteen, he joined the United States Marine Corps.

My dad never talks about his past, so I know about this only from bits and pieces my mom has told me. He keeps his darker emotions to himself, which is something I've inherited from him. Maybe if he'd learned to deal with his own childhood pain, he might have been able to help me with mine.

My mom, Jazzlyn, has had a life full of trauma as well. She was raised Southern Baptist in Wagoner, Oklahoma, the middle child sandwiched by an older brother, Doug, and a younger sister, Stacy. She was a rugged tomboy as a little kid but grew into one of the most popular girls in school, a beautiful cheerleader with long black hair and sultry green eyes. All the boys wanted to date her, and all the girls wanted to be her. That her family was relatively well off, and owned fancy cars and horses, didn't hurt either. She was the queen bee, a bit of a "mean girl" who ruthlessly made fun of gay and handicapped people. But despite her glory at school, life at home was hell. Her father was a cruel alcoholic who verbally and physically abused his wife and children daily. He was incredibly strict and would beat them if orders weren't followed, sometimes even when they were. When he died in a construction crane accident when my mom was thirteen, she was sad but also relieved.

At eighteen Mom married her first husband and gave birth to a son, Derik. Derik's dad cheated on her relentlessly, though, and after a couple of years they divorced. When Derik was three, she married again and gave birth to her second son, Josh, who was born with a condition called agenesis of the corpus callosum—malformation of the fibers that connect the two hemispheres of the brain—which in

Josh's case caused severe mental disability. Mom's husband told her she had to put Josh up for adoption or he was going to leave. My mom, renouncing her bigot ways, loved Josh with all her heart and told her husband to get the hell out.

Josh wasn't expected to live more than a few days, but he survived—though he was extremely handicapped. My mom tried to raise both Josh and Derik on her own, but she struggled to make enough money to cover Josh's medical expenses and Derik's hyperactivity disorder. When Derik was four, it was decided that the best thing for him would be for his father to raise him.

Meanwhile, despite all the doctors' predictions, Josh continued to live. When he was a few months old, there was an article about him in the local Wagoner paper, calling his continued survival a miracle. The article showed pictures of my mom playing with Josh and praised her for being a devoted mother. What my mom didn't know was that a man read the article and became obsessed with her. He stalked her for months until one day he broke into her apartment and raped her at knifepoint, slashing her with the knife and threatening to kill Josh if she didn't do as he wanted. When he left, my mom crawled her way to her phone and called her brother, who called the police. The police came and took her to the hospital.

The police found her attacker's bloody footprints, which led them to a trailer park five blocks away. When they opened the door to his trailer, they found the walls covered in photographs of my mom, like something out of *Law & Order: Special Victims Unit*. The man was arrested and sentenced to 175 years in prison. His family threatened to kill my mom,

so she was put into witness protection and legally changed her name. From the time I was about twelve I'd known my mom had been raped, but it wasn't until a year ago—when I opened the mail to find documents from the prison, updating my mom on the man's continued incarceration—that she told me what had actually happened.

After the rape my mom fell into depression. She was struggling with money and struggling to take care of Josh, and one night she decided she was going to kill herself. She had just started dating my dad, and when he wasn't home, she went into his apartment, got his gun, and got down on her knees, crying, prepared to kill Josh and then herself. She didn't want Josh to have to grow up in a world that wouldn't love him as much as she did. She didn't do it, though. She called my dad, and he came and got her and took her to get help.

Josh was put into a children's hospital where he could get twenty-four-hour care, and my mom started therapy to deal with being raped and her pain over the separation from Derik and Josh. Meanwhile she and my dad grew closer.

I don't know if my parents were ever truly in love. My mom has told me she wonders if my dad just wanted to rescue her because he had been abandoned as a child, and if likewise she'd just wanted the protection her father had never given her. Whatever the reasons, my dad proposed— he promised to take care of her and give her a comfortable life, and she promised to give him children and be a good wife. They married in Las Vegas on July 28, 1993. My mom was in her late twenties and had braces at the time, which makes for a pretty funny wedding photo. For their honeymoon they took off on a forty-five-day road trip, and in the freezing cold mountains of Canada, I was conceived. My mom tells me those first few years of their marriage were the happiest of her life. When the Oklahoma City bombing happened, she tried to be there for my dad, and for a while he let her. But his drinking had begun, and she wouldn't be able to hold him for much longer.

Unlike my dad, my mom never stopped fighting to try to do what was best for her children. She's the strongest woman I know, and I can't imagine having lived her life. After everything both my parents had been through, I know that all they wanted was to raise a happy, healthy child. I wish I could have expressed to them what was going on with me as I grew estranged from my body and didn't understand my place in the world at such a young age. It could have saved what would turn into more than a decade of pain. But how could I explain it to them, when I barely understood it myself?

6

When I was five, my dad was assigned to a military base in Fort Lauderdale, Florida. My brother Jake had been born a year earlier, and Josh was still living in a residential facility for handicapped people in North Carolina, which my mom visited regularly.

We moved into a really nice, big house in Pembroke Pines, and I was enrolled in the local elementary, Silver Palms, a fancy, uppity school with uniforms and rigorous academics. I was nervous about starting at a new school—I had left behind a bunch of good friends in Japan—but happily, I almost immediately liked Silver Palms. Even though I knew something was "off" with my body, gender itself wasn't an issue. Sure, I had some feminine characteristics—like crossing my legs when I sat, or talking with my hands—but at that age a kid's gender isn't really scrutinized. It's considered okay for children to act ambiguous—little boys can play with dolls and little girls can roughhouse, and adults don't think too much of it.

After school I'd spend the afternoons playing with the

other kids in my neighborhood. My best friend was a stocky kid named Deon. We'd play with action figures, climb trees, play video games, or just chase each other around on our bikes—pretty classic "boy" activities. Sometimes we'd hang out with this tomboyish girl named Emma. Emma was the only girl our age in the neighborhood, but she fit right in with the boys. She loved roughhousing and sports and killing ants. (For the record, I was *not* into killing ants.) As far as I knew, no one judged Emma for being tomboyish, and no one questioned my occasional "girl" proclivities, like when I asked for an Easy-Bake oven for my birthday or when I would play dress-up and dance around in my mom's high heels.

Often trans narratives might focus on how—in the case of a male-to-female, for instance—a child born male loved pink, or only wanted to play house, and this is used to "prove" the child's true female identity. I want to be clear that my love of stereotypical girl toys, such as my Easy-Bake oven or my baby doll that magically looked like it was actually drinking milk, is not what makes me female. Frankly, I think all little boys would like playing house and dress-up if they gave it a shot. What makes me female is something I felt in the core of myself: that my external body did not match up with how I felt inside, and that I was being seen by others as something I was not. I know this can be a difficult, abstract concept if it's not your personal experience, but it was mine.

This feeling was most prominent around places like the swimming pool. I looked at the girls in their one-piece suits and wished I could wear those too. It didn't feel right for me to take my shirt off like the boys, and even though everyone urged me to, from the age of six on, I refused. It wasn't that I knew I was a girl. It was just that, for some reason, taking off my shirt made me uncomfortable, as if people shouldn't be looking at that part of my body. I'd watch the girls jumping around in their brightly colored suits and wish I could be graceful, pretty, and carefree like them, not stuck in my ugly boy trunks and T-shirt.

Similarly, I always admired the earrings the girls at Silver Palms wore. I had some older friends, boys, who had gotten one ear pierced, and I convinced my parents that everyone was doing it and I should have my ear pierced too. I told them I needed to get my left ear pierced because that was how you let people know you were straight and not gay.

"I don't know, Luke. You're only six," my mom said. "What do you think, Randy?"

"*Why* does he want to get his ear pierced?" asked my dad.

"I need to get it pierced so people know I'm straight!" I pleaded.

"Oh, all right . . . if it means that much to you," my mom said.

It's pretty ridiculous, but I essentially used homophobia to get my ear pierced like the girls and to express my burgeoning transgenderism. By making my parents think I didn't want to be seen as gay, I was able to feel a little more like a girl.

In fact, age six was when I first noticed my attraction to boys. Some days I would go to an after-school program with kids from all different grades. Boys my own age were uninteresting, but I found myself having new, exciting feelings for several of the fifth- and sixth-grade boys. There was one boy named Matt who had tan skin and a large nose, and who always wore polo shirts. I developed my first real crush on him. I remember sitting at the computer next to him, both of us playing a game, and me trying to come up with questions to ask him.

"I can't get past this level! How did you do it?"

"Here. I'll beat it for you," Matt would say, leaning in and taking over my keypad for a moment.

When he spoke to me, I'd get a tingling rush like I'd never felt before. A small part of me knew that my feelings were "gay" or "wrong," but I was so young that these worries were vague, unformed, and didn't really cause me much anxiety.

All in all, despite my discomfort with my body and the stirrings of confusion over my attraction to boys, I was a relatively happy kid in Florida. I loved learning at school, and my dad and I were still close. Every Friday night he and I would walk to the day care center across the street from our house and play tennis. He was always patient with me, not caring when it took almost an hour for me to just hit the ball over the net. I didn't really like tennis—I was clumsy at sports in general—but I would tell him I wanted to stay and keep playing, because it meant more time with him. Eventually the sun would start to set, and we'd walk back to our house, watching the palm trees sway in the warm Florida air.

"You'll be a pro in no time," he'd say, ruffling my hair. "Tomorrow we should try a little football."

Ugh, football! I'd think.

"Okay, Daddy. And maybe after football we could just ride bikes?" I didn't like sports but was naturally good at bike riding, and adored it. You couldn't keep me off my bike.

"Why not?" my dad would say. "We've got the whole weekend." And he'd give me a squeeze. It never occurred to me that our bond could be broken, or that my confidence and general sense of peace could ever change.

I didn't know that when I turned seven and we moved to Oklahoma, the darkness would descend.

7

FAR FROM OKAY IN OKAY

We were still in Florida when my dad got PCS (permanent change of station) orders to move to Washington, DC. He and my mom sat down to talk about it, and he said he didn't want to play the political game there. Meanwhile my mom's mother and her boyfriend were putting pressure on us to move back to Oklahoma so they could be near Jake and me.

"Look," my dad told my mom one night at dinner, "I'm lieutenant colonel. Why don't I just retire? Even though I hate Oklahoma, let's move back there and let your parents enjoy being grandparents."

"Let's do it," said my mom.

Ten days after we moved to Oklahoma, 9/11 happened. If we had moved to DC, my dad's office would have been in the Pentagon, where six of his friends were killed. He was devastated. As for my grandma and her boyfriend, whom I knew as Grandpa, they separated within months of us moving there. Neither of them ended up being involved in Jake's and my life.

Okay, Oklahoma, is a small, rural town with a population of only six hundred twenty. In Florida most of the kids I'd known had been other military brats, and everyone had been well-off. I remember looking around the flat, dusty expanse of Okay and seeing mostly broken-down vehicles in front of small, ramshackle houses and trailers. There was one hamburger joint, one gas station, and as far as I could tell, not much else. I would soon learn that my family was the richest in town. We lived in a large, white, two-story house with a pool out back, while the other kids all lived in trailers or small houses. Our house was right on the water of Sequoyah Bay, where we could go boating and swimming.

When I started school, I was shocked by how small it was. The entire elementary school was fewer than a hundred kids, and we were all crammed into one small building and a gym. The playground was decent, with jungle gyms, monkey bars, slides, and a merry-go-round. But shortly after I arrived, the merry-go-round would be dismantled after a kid cracked his skull open on it.

Compared to the advanced academics of Silver Palms Elementary in Florida, Okay was at a standstill. In the first grade at Silver Palms, we'd been learning multiplication, division, and the chemistry concept of buoyancy. In second grade in Okay everyone seemed to be amazed that four plus three equals seven. Most of the teachers were actually sports coaches who needed to teach a class in order to keep their jobs.

As I began second grade, the divide between boys and girls became increasingly prominent. Living in that ambiguous, genderless space of early childhood ceased to be an option. Boys who played with dolls were now laughed at or looked at with suspicion, and girls were expected to gleefully run away when boys chased them on the playground for a kiss. When I realized that my feminine characteristics—the graceful way I walked, my girlish voice—were now being judged and I was expected to align myself with the boys, depression swiftly overtook me. My Florida tan faded into a clammy white, and dark bags formed under my eyes as I became increasingly withdrawn. I wasn't comfortable in my body and felt like everyone was scrutinizing me, so I tried not to be seen at all. Within months of moving I rarely changed my clothes, rarely bathed, rarely ate, and would leave the house only if forced to. When my parents made me go out to dinner with them, I would insist on hiding under the table at the restaurant, where no one could see me. I would sit down there, drawing or coloring, eating—if anything—a plastic baggie of Goldfish crackers my mom would bring from home.

I desperately wanted my mom or dad to help me, to somehow make me feel better, but I didn't know how to ask. I didn't know if it was my being feminine or depressed or both, but every day my dad seemed to be pulling further away from me. He began to favor Jake, buying him endless presents—toys, bikes, video games, four-wheelers—and stopped caring to ever get anything for me. At first I would ask for things, but when the answer was always no, I eventually stopped asking.

One night I was lying in bed, just staring at the ceiling, a feeling of dread spreading over my body, when my mom came in to say good night. She brushed away my bangs to kiss my forehead, and I started crying.

"Mom?" I said, looking into her warm, familiar face.

"What's wrong?" she said, smoothing my hair. Her eyes looked worried, but more than that, they looked scared.

"Why do I exist?"

"What do you mean?"

"What's the point?" I said, rubbing at my tears with my fists. "There isn't a point to life. I wish I was dead."

My mom climbed onto my bed and hugged me tight. "What are you talking about, sweetie? Don't say that."

I only cried harder.

A few days later my mom sat me down.

"Honey, your dad and I talked, and we think it's a good idea for you to talk with someone about what you're feeling."

I was immediately filled with dread, and as it turned out, rightly so. My parents proceeded to bring me to a string of psychiatrists who started me on endless rounds of medication. Between the ages of seven and nine I was put on Zoloft, Cymbalta, Adderall, Xanax, and Prozac. The doctors would try one or two months on one, and when I didn't show any signs of improvement, they'd increase the dose. And when that didn't work, they'd try the next one. Each medication only made me feel more depressed. I don't know whether this was because the drugs negatively affected my brain chemistry or if I was just depressed they weren't working. Either way, the more we tried, the more frustrated I became that nothing seemed to "fix" me.

I remember one therapist in particular whom I saw when I was eight. His name was Dr. Ashman, and we would drive over to the next town, Muskogee, to see him. His office was in a small, sandstone-colored building with an incredibly tiny waiting room, where I remember watching the secretary with her flamboyant hairdo, typing away at an astonishing speed. I'd usually chat with her before I went in to see Dr. Ashman, and her calm voice always made me feel warm and welcome. Dr. Ashman was a different story.

As soon as I walked into his office, I'd be hit by this musky odor that made me feel congested and like I couldn't breathe. There was a large, darkly colored rug that made the shadowy room feel even darker. On his wooden desk sat an American flag and some old fountain pens and pads of paper. Behind the desk was a giant bookshelf lined with books and framed photos of his family. His office always seemed more like a study to write books in than a place to try to help children. He would sit on a dark blue couch while I sat in a matching blue recliner. He was a tall man with thick glasses, and he wore only dark suits with weird mismatched ties. I would stare at his black shoes, which always seemed to be dusty.

The first time I saw Dr. Ashman, I lay down on the recliner, looked up at the ceiling, and thought, *This time is going to be different. This therapist will know what is wrong with me and how to help.* I had already seen a handful of therapists—but most of them had been psychiatrists, there only to prescribe medication. I'd see them for one session, they'd put me on some new antidepressant, and then when the

antidepressant failed, I'd see them maybe once more, sometimes never again. But this time my mom told me I was in
therapy just to talk, not to get medicine, so I decided to tell
Dr. Ashman what I had never spoken aloud to anyone else.

"I feel like a girl in a boy's body. And I want to die," I
told him.

Dr. Ashman just nodded and jotted down notes. For the
next several sessions I continued trying to connect with him,
to express as best I could everything I was feeling, that my
suicidal thoughts were real. But he never spoke back to me,
never tried to help me understand these problems or figure
out how to fix them, only nodded and wrote down more
notes. His nonresponsiveness caused me to feel even lone-
lier, and by the fifth session I decided I would try another
tack. Since he wasn't paying attention to what I was saying,
I would get him to pay attention by telling him what he
wanted to hear.

I stopped saying how depressed I was and that I didn't
understand whether I was a boy or a girl, and began manip-
ulating him. It was slow at first—I knew if I completely
switched my attitude, he would be suspicious. So I started
small, smiling more and asking him questions about his life.
Gradually I began to sit and talk differently. I knew boys
talked with more confidence, that they used a certain tone
girls lacked, and that they sat reclined with their legs wide
open. I was aware that people thought sissy boys were that
way from being too close with their mothers, so I told him
how I loved playing sports with my dad (who, in reality, I
barely saw anymore), how football was just the most awesome thing ever. My goal was to convince Ashman that I was

"cured" so I would never have to see him or any other therapist again. The key to this convincing was in the details—it's
the little things that make the lie. I know it's not something I should be proud of, but lying is a skill I developed
and honed from an early age, and would continue to use
throughout my life.

My manipulation of Ashman worked. He eventually
told my parents there was nothing wrong with me. I was a
healthy, happy, normal eight-year-old boy.

"In fact," my mom told me, as she drove me home from
my last session with Ashman, "he suggested that maybe
Daddy and I should come in for some counseling."

"He did?" I asked, a little stunned. That had not been
my intention.

"What I want to know," my mom said, looking at me—
not exactly cross, but more confused to the point of frus-
tration, "is how he can think you're so happy, when you're
miserable at home?"

"I don't know. . . . I guess he's a bad doctor," I said, staring out the window.

I would find out later that Dr. Ashman told my mom he
thought I was so well adjusted that his professional assess-
ment was that my parents were projecting their own neuro-
ses onto me. He told my mom she "wanted" something to
be wrong with me the way there was something wrong with
her other son, Josh, but unlike with Josh, she might be able
to fix me. He thought my dad's problems stemmed from
parenting too late in life. I had no idea my manipulations
would go so far.

Meanwhile, my self-hating darkness only grew. I didn't

understand why I had to live in the body I had. I longed to grow my hair out and to wear beautiful colors, and was filled with torturous envy of every beautiful woman I saw.

At school the teacher would drone on at the front of the room while I hunched into my chair and hurled insults at myself inside my brain.

You're ugly. You're idiotic. You're foolish, I said to myself, over and over. I'd look around at the other kids. They appeared so happy and carefree, waving their hands, answering questions, whispering when the teacher wasn't looking. Why couldn't I be like them? I looked back down at my hands, balled into fists in my lap. *No one will ever love you,* I told myself. It was as if there were a demon inside me, spitting on me, mocking me in order to drive me further into hopelessness.

One night when I was eight, after a year of contemplating suicide, I decided to do it. It was the Fourth of July and I was inside the house, alone, listening to the laughter and voices of my mom, dad, brother, aunts, and uncles outside as they celebrated and set off fireworks. I was jealous of their bliss, how easily happiness came to them, while everything seemed sad and uninteresting to me.

I drew a knife from the kitchen block and locked myself in the bathroom. I sat on a stool and stared at the knife in my hand, crying silently. I didn't care whether my parents would be upset by my death. I just wanted the pain to end. I thought about how after I was gone my depression would no longer be a burden to my parents and I wouldn't have to compete with my little brother for affection. It was clear: the best thing, for me and for the rest of the world, was to just cut my wrist. My hand grasping the knife shook and quivered as I searched for the strength to move it, but it was as if some strong force were holding my arm, forcing me to keep the knife still.

I sat there like that for more than an hour. The fireworks continued to boom outside. As much as I wanted to do it, something in my body was stopping me. Finally I dropped the knife and started cursing and screaming in anger. I went back into the kitchen, threw the knife into the block in a fuss, and ran to my room. I cried myself to sleep that night, listening to the fireworks and party go on. No one came to check on me.

8

IMMORTAL BLOOD

By the time I was nine and entering the fourth grade, I was fully aware that I was a girl trapped in a boy's body. I didn't know that transgenderism existed, though, so all that knowledge meant to me was that I was doomed.

I was also, at this age, very certain of my attraction to boys. Even though I never spoke my feelings out loud, because of my feminine appearance and behavior, everyone else assumed I was gay, which, in a conservative state like Oklahoma, is not an okay thing to be. At school I was teased relentlessly. Kids poked fun at my delicate features and stick-thin body. Rumors floated around that I took ballet and that I got the first-place award for being "the gayest kid in the world." I would even catch the teachers snickering to one another when I walked by.

There was one boy I had the hugest crush on. His name was Brian, and though he was my age, he could have passed for much older. Brian wasn't too into sports, but he liked horsing around outside. Often when I was hanging around the girls on the playground, he'd run up to me and start a game of tag.

"Luke's It!" he'd say, and I'd be excited just to have him touch me.

The thing is, even though I was infatuated with Brian and several guy TV stars, I knew I wasn't "gay." I didn't want boys to like me back as a boy. I wanted them to like me as a girl. The thought of a boy liking me as a boy was horrifying. The thought made me feel disgusted, panicked, and trapped. It was as if a guy liking me as a guy would affirm my identity as male—which I knew I wasn't. But because I didn't know transgenderism existed, "gay" was the only word I had to describe what made me feel different. One night I decided to tell my mom. My dad was up in his den, Jake had gone to sleep, and it was just me and my mom, watching TV on the couch.

"Mom . . . ?"

"Mm-hm?" she said, her eyes still on the TV.

I could feel my heart racing and a sickening feeling taking over me, but I plowed ahead anyway. I just needed to get this out.

"I feel attracted to some of the guys at school. I think I might be gay."

My mom picked up the remote and turned down the sound on the TV. She looked at me and smiled. It was a nervous smile, though. I could tell she was uncomfortable.

"That's okay," she said. "We'll figure it out."

Figure it out? I wasn't really sure what she meant by that.

"I'm scared," I said. "I—I feel confused. . . ."

"Everything's going to be fine," she said. Then she picked

up the remote, turned the sound back up, and turned her face back to the TV.

The next morning it was as if I'd never come out at all. I thought maybe my mom would bring it up again, suggest we talk about it some more, or ask how I felt, but she never did. I almost wondered if I'd even told her at all. I figured she must have just forgotten, and I was too ashamed to bring it up again.

I decided to try talking to Andy. Andy was one of the few close friends I had my entire time in Okay. He was a sweet kid whose face jiggled when he walked. The times goofing around with Andy are some of my only happy memories from that period. We would spend hours play-fighting and pretending to cast spells from *Harry Potter*. I could be myself around Andy, as girly and feminine as I wanted, and he couldn't have cared less. To him I was still a boy—it didn't register that there was anything wrong with the way I crossed my legs when I sat, or talked with my hands or bounced around.

One day during recess Andy and I were hanging out on the swings, when I worked up the nerve to tell him.

"So . . . this is kinda weird," I said, "but I think Brian is cute."

"Oh. Okay," said Andy.

Just then our friends Jody and Mercedes walked up.

"What are you guys talking about?" asked Jody.

Andy glanced at me.

Just tell them, I said to myself. "I think Brian is cute," I said.

"Brian *is* cute," said Jody.

"Wait, you *do?*" asked Mercedes. She gave me a kind of cockeyed smile.

"Yeah," I said. And then, in a panicked moment of nervousness, I just started lying. "Also, I was just telling Andy how last weekend I was hanging out with Daniel Radcliffe, Emma Watson, and Rupert Grint. They were in town on their way to shoot the next movie." We were all obsessed with the actors from the Harry Potter movies.

"*Really?*" Jody asked.

"You're lying," said Mercedes.

"Wait, did you really?" asked Andy.

"It's true. And you want to know something else?" I said with a tone of gravitas.

They all leaned in close, eager to listen.

"I'm not really a boy."

Jody gasped.

"Yeah," I continued. "I have to wear this boy-mask because my mom wanted a boy. But I'm actually really a girl."

"Whoa . . . ," said Andy.

Then we all started laughing because it was just so absurd.

"*Locomotor mortis!*" Andy exclaimed, waving his stick-wand at us. We all stuck our legs together and began hopping around.

"*Obscuro!*" I exclaimed, waving my stick-wand at Andy. Andy promptly closed his eyes, stumbling around, pretending to be blindfolded.

I wonder if covering up the truth about my being attracted to Brian—by lying that I knew the cast of Harry Potter and wore a boy-mask—made it so my friends didn't know what to believe. Whatever they thought, my friends, like my mom, never brought up my confessions again.

It didn't matter how many times or to whom I tried to come out—it was like what I said just disappeared the next day. And that's how I felt, too. Like I just wanted to disappear. My mom put my fourth-grade group class photo in her scrapbook, but when you search for me in the rows of kids, all you find is a hole cut out where my face should be.

While I didn't want anyone to look at my body, I did have confidence in my intelligence, and since I needed something to grab on to in life, I decided to be the very best in school. Much like an athlete strives to be the best in his sport, I forced myself to learn every strand of information I could.

At ten I was already reading at a twelfth-grade level. I joined the Accelerated Reader program at school and racked up so many points in so little time for all the books I read that I was the focus of an article about the program in the *Muskogee Phoenix*, the local newspaper. "Luke always has been a voracious reader," my mom is quoted as saying. "The thicker the book the better. He was reading before he even knew what an Accelerated Reader point was." I was so thrilled when the article came out that for a few days I actually thought, *Maybe I'm okay. Maybe I will be okay.* I read the article out loud to my mom so many times, we each had it memorized, and even my dad seemed proud of me again. Of course, after about a week the excitement of the article died down, and I searched for something else to feel good about as I felt the hopelessness and self-hate creeping back.

I knew a few kids in my class who had diabetes, and I soon became obsessed with finding a cure. I had decided I wanted to be a pathologist when I grew up—but why wait? I was convinced that if I just worked hard enough, I could find the cure for diabetes now. I spent hours researching and writing about the pancreas, insulin, and the beta cells of the islets of Langerhans, searching for potential cures. I just wanted—needed—to feel good about myself. I was determined to leave my mark on the world.

It was great to have academics as a source of pride, but there were also downsides. I gained a reputation as a know-it-all and smarty-pants, one more reason for my classmates to dislike me (unless I was helping them with their homework). And there was my unfortunate behavior in class. I became utterly unable to tolerate failure, a problem I'll admit I still have to this day. If a teacher praised another student instead of me or I received a ghastly B on a test, I would burst into tears and collapse onto my desk, sobbing in despair. My mom grew used to receiving calls from the teacher: "Luke is having another nervous breakdown." I could not bear the idea of any student doing better than me. School was the one thing I was good at, and if I couldn't be the absolute best, it meant I was worthless.

In addition to schoolwork, the other way I was able to tolerate living was by immersing myself in books and movies. I became fixated on any story that was magical. In retrospect I imagine this was motivated by my longing to magically transform my own body. Locked alone in my room, I devoured the Harry Potter series, the Chronicles of Narnia, and the Lord of the Rings trilogy. My favorite movies were Disney's *The Little Mermaid*—I related to Ariel's desire to be something else—and *Matilda*, based on the Roald Dahl book, about a little girl with neglectful parents who discovers she has telekinetic powers. Some weekend mornings I would just sit and watch *Matilda* over and over.

Inspired by all the fantasy books I was reading, I devoted myself to the creation of my own magical world—a book series called the Rainfall Trilogy. By the time I stopped working on it, it was more than eight hundred pages long. I started out writing it longhand, but when my mom found some of the pages, she had me switch to her laptop so she could save my writing on flash drives. I didn't plan any of the story out. I would just sit down and think, *What do I want to write today?* Essentially it was a kind of diary. You can chart my emotions going up and down through the characters' adventures and struggles.

The heroine is Rain—half human girl, half immortal elf—and she was my beautiful, brave alter ego. At one point in the story, Rain fails to protect the king's son and is sentenced to death. The king is then told by order of the Dragon Council that he can't execute Rain because high elves are an endangered species—having been hunted for centuries for their immortal blood—and Rain is the last of her kind. So instead the king casts Rain into a tomb of stone and throws her into the ocean, where she remains trapped but alive for hundreds of years.

When I think about it now, the story is such an obvious parallel to how I felt at the time. Like Rain—a rare, endangered species—I felt like I was a different species than the people around me. Everyone else seemed so comfortable in their gender, while I knew that I did not match up with mine. Likewise, Rain being trapped in a tomb of stone expressed how I felt in my skin, as if I were literally trapped in a box the exact size and shape of my body. Every movement, every breath I took, felt constricted because I knew my body was wrong.

Shut away in my room reading, writing, or researching diabetes, I was barely a part of my family. But in many ways we were hardly a family anyway. My brother Jake and I never played, only bickered and taunted each other, sometimes shoving and hitting. Any little thing could set us off—whose turn it was to pick a TV show to watch or who ate the last bag of potato chips in the house. He'd bite himself and then cry to our mom that I had done it. Often I wished I had. If we weren't fighting, we'd just ignore each other. My mom and dad barely spoke. Sometimes they'd go into their bedroom, and I would hear muffled fighting. Once, I listened in at the door and heard my dad say something like, "I don't want a sissy for a son."

It's my fault, I thought. *Everyone would be happier if I didn't exist.*

My mom burst out of the bedroom and was startled to see me standing there.

"Is everything okay?" I asked.

"Everything's fine," she said, and walked past me.

These instances of fighting were rare, though. Mostly, like Jake and I did, my mom and dad just ignored each other. My dad would come home from work and go straight to his den, where he'd spend the night drinking until he passed out. My mom and Jake would eat dinner together, and after they went to bed, I'd venture out of my room to pick at the food my mom had left for me in the microwave. Sometimes I'd take a bath—though I despised this activity because it forced me to be aware of my body. Usually I'd tuck my penis between my legs so I wouldn't have to look at it.

Even though I was doing well in fourth grade and had found a few friends, my feelings of despair didn't fade. I would often think of that day in the bathroom when I was eight, holding the knife to my wrist. My face would burn with shame, thinking of my cowardice. I didn't want fear to stop me the way it had that Fourth of July night, so I concocted what I saw as a foolproof plan: I was going to drown myself by tying cinder blocks to my body and jumping into our pool.

One sunny afternoon when I was home alone, I drifted into the backyard. With all my strength I lifted four cinder blocks, one by one, into my dad's wheelbarrow. I then tangled and twisted a rope through and around the blocks and wrapped the rope tight around my wrist. I tugged at the restraint to make sure there was no way my hand or the ropes could come loose. I then hunched over, picked up the wheelbarrow handles, and headed down to our pool.

At the pool's edge I tipped the wheelbarrow over so that the blocks fell to the ground. Without hesitating I then climbed into the pool and with a sharp tug brought the cinder blocks in with me. I sank, just as expected, and also just as expected, I panicked. My mind was bent on suicide, but my body involuntarily struggled, pulling and yanking at the thick rope. Then a strange calm took over me, and it was as if my body had finally given in, a fatal victim to my mind.

But when I opened my eyes, to my horror and surprise the entire rope around the cinder blocks had untangled and I was floating freely at the surface of the water. I took a large gasp of air and cursed myself once again. *You can't even kill yourself properly.*

In hindsight I wonder if there was a part of me that, despite all my pain, did not want to die, and maybe that small part didn't tie the rope as tightly as I should have. Also, as suicidal as I was, I thought killing yourself was a mortal sin that could land you in hell for eternity—a prospect that terrified me. In fact, much of my fear and confusion at this time was related to my being a Christian.

My dad was raised Mormon, my mom Southern Baptist, and a belief in God and Christian values was taken as a given in our family. Oklahoma is the buckle of the Bible Belt, so these beliefs were everywhere around me as well. Like most people I knew, I imagined God as a man with a beard in the clouds looking down. The more I learned about him, the more I grew to fear him.

When I was ten, my mom enrolled me in a summer Christian church program. Every day I got up and got dressed, and my mom would drive me to an enormous activity center where I and about thirty other kids did arts and crafts, played sports, ate lunch, and for three one-hour sessions throughout the day prayed and discussed the Bible. The games I liked, and the sports I put up with, but the forced praying and Bible discussions only intensified my growing terror of God. During these sessions the adult and teenage supervisors would go into explicit detail about everything that God considered deviant—in particular homosexuality, which at the time I had accepted as the closest thing to whatever I was. Though my parents were Christian, at home they didn't discuss God openly too often, and we didn't pray before meals or anything.

But at this camp I came to see God as a very real, omnipotent, omniscient force of wrath and anger. He punished the wicked and rewarded the good, and with the way I felt about my body and my attraction to boys, there was no question which side I fell on. I was terrified for my salvation. At home, alone in my room, I would sit and read the Leviticus chapter of the Bible, obsessing over the passages on sinful sexual behavior, such as, "If a man practices homosexuality, having sex with another man as with a woman, both men have committed a detestable act. They must both be put to death, for they are guilty of a capital offense." I'd read that passage over and over, giving myself chills of fear.

One day I was sitting in a Bible session at camp when Sebastian, the boy next to me who had become somewhat of a friend, stared at me and said, "You look so much like a girl to me."

"Oh, well . . . I *am* a girl!" I said in a hushed tone back.

His eyes grew to the size of golf balls. Similar to the time when I told Andy, Jody, and Mercedes that I was a girl, I felt a rush at having spoken what I knew deep down to be the truth. It was absurd, though, because we all knew, on the surface, that this couldn't possibly be true. Sebastian laughed nervously, and I did too, and then we both turned back to whatever Bible verse the adult was ranting on about.

On another day, the teenagers told us how Jesus sweat blood when he begged God to not let him be crucified. I

7

remember feeling so sorry for Jesus, sorry he'd had to endure such pain and beg God, his father, to spare him. The way they told the story made me swell with emotion, and for just a second I felt as if Jesus and I had something in common. I began to cry, and the teenagers monitoring the discussion ran over.

"This child is feeling the Holy Spirit!" they declared. "This boy has become saved!"

They kept me after the session and gave me a little button that read I WAS SAVED TODAY!

I didn't want to correct them and say that I wasn't crying because I felt as though God were looking over me. For just a moment I had felt as though I'd been in Jesus's shoes . . . or sandals.

My mom tried to get me to go back to the Christian camp the following summer, but I refused. The older and unhappier I became, the more strained my relationship with God was. It just didn't make sense to me that an all-knowing, benevolent force would make my life so miserable.

"You just have to trust in God," my mom would say. "He *does* love you, and he *is* looking over you."

"God hates me," I'd say under my breath.

My mom would just shake her head, choosing to ignore what I said because she didn't like it, rather than help me understand my feelings.

Many of the kids at school also couldn't comprehend what I possibly had to be depressed about. To them I was the envied rich kid, the boy who lived in the fancy house with a pool, Jacuzzi, motorcycles, and sprawling gardens. Despite being mostly teased and rejected, when my birthday came around and I started handing out Power Rangers invitations for my party, suddenly all the kids wanted to be my friend. I knew their attention was fleeting, but I still couldn't help basking in it while it lasted.

My twelfth birthday party was one of the greatest days of my life. It felt like the entire school was crammed into my backyard as my dad flipped burgers and hot dogs, we sang karaoke, and then all the kids cannonballed into the pool. I was especially excited because Brian—the boy I'd had an intense crush on for three years—was there. He wore baggy blue swim trunks and looked amazing flexing his muscles, splashing around in the pool.

"Luke! Why are you swimming in a T-shirt?" he asked with a laugh.

"I don't know," I said, blushing.

"Well, it's your birthday. You can do what you want!" he said, and then lunged at me with a giant splash.

Later that night most of the kids had gone home, but Brian still hadn't been picked up. We were playing video games and eating leftover cold hot dogs. I didn't want him to leave.

"Hey, maybe you could sleep over?" I asked.

"Cool!"

My mom called his mom, and the next thing I knew, Brian—*Brian!*—was spending the night. We stayed up late in my room playing *Pool Paradise*, a billiards game on PlayStation, and just generally fooling around. At one point he tried to grab my controller from me, and we fell to the floor wrestling. Feeling his body on top of mine felt good in a way I had never experienced before. He felt something too, because before I knew it, we weren't just wrestling anymore. We were rubbing into each other, moving our hips and breathing heavily. I'm not sure how it ended—one of us rolled off and we picked up our video game controllers as if nothing had happened.

"Get ready to have your ass whupped," said Brian as we restarted our game.

"You wish," I said, and stared at the TV, my body still tingling from what had just happened. I thought, *Oh my God, I'm going to hell.*

That Monday at school it was as if nothing had happened. Brian wasn't mean to me, he wasn't nice, he wasn't weird, he wasn't anything. We went back to being casual friends as if the entire experience had been wiped from his brain. In a way this relieved me. I didn't want to think about it either. I knew that what had happened was "wrong." As much as I tried to forget it, though, I couldn't. My anxiety about my sexuality intensified. It had been a couple of years since I'd tried to tell my mom I was gay. I decided I needed to try to tell her again.

That day when she picked me up in the car from school, I just blurted it out.

"Mom, I'm attracted to Brian, and that scares me. I think I'm gay."

My mom looked over at me and put her hand on my shoulder. "That's okay. It's gonna be all right." She looked back out at the road.

I started crying. "It's not all right," I said. "The thing is, I don't even want him to like me back as a boy. . . . I can't stand the thought of him liking me as a boy. Does that make any sense?"

"It's going to be fine," she said. "How about Lukie burgers for dinner?" Lukie burgers were what we called sloppy joes because I loved them so much.

"Yeah, sure," I said. I stared down at my feet.

About six months later, in the middle of seventh grade, my family moved to Bixby, another Oklahoma town about an hour away. After retiring from the military, my dad had taken a job as a JROTC (Junior Reserve Officer Training Corps) instructor at Bixby High School. The commute was getting to be too much for him, so he and my mom decided we should move. The day we left, my mom picked me up at school during lunchtime. Everyone was hanging out in the small yard between the gym and the high school, and as her car pulled up, I shouted, "HEY, EVERYONE! I'M LEAVING FOREVER!" And all the kids—even the ones who had teased me the most—ran over to give me hugs good-bye and wish me luck.

And leaving forever I was. Three years later "Luke" would cease to exist.

9

THE MAGIC WORD

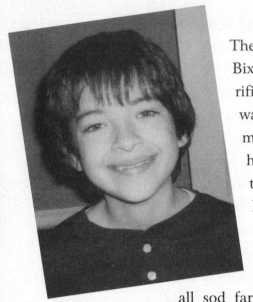

The first day I walked into Bixby Middle School, I was terrified. The lunchroom at Bixby was larger than the *entire* Okay middle school. In Okay there had been only thirty kids in the middle school to get to know. Now I was faced with a class of more than four hundred strangers.

Bixby was originally all sod farming, but in the past ten years it has boomed, and it is now a desirable suburb for professionals working in Tulsa to drive home to at night. One of the reasons it became so popular is its middle and high schools—particularly the athletic programs, where the majority of money is funneled. Students don't always have enough books, but they do have a 1.5-million-dollar football field. Like the characters on the beloved television show *Friday Night Lights*, the football players in Bixby are treated like gods. Suffice it to say, it was not the greatest place for a rail-thin, glasses-wearing, gender-variant twelve-year-old such as myself.

I scanned the lunchroom, trying to figure out the best

place to sit. I was scared to sit near any boys, worried they might start teasing and harassing me. I spotted a table with three girls who appeared welcoming. They weren't exceedingly attractive or wearing fancy clothes, which made them seem approachable. Still, I was way too shy to introduce myself, so I sat at the edge of their table and quietly opened my lunch. *"Hey! Are you new? You seem like you'd be nice to talk to!"* I imagined one of them saying. But of course they didn't even notice that I had sat down.

As I ate, I watched them out of the corner of my eye. One of the girls had blond hair and wore a bright blue hoodie and jeans. Her voice sounded sweet and excited as she thumbed through her binder, showing the others drawings she had done. I turned my head slightly to get a better look. She'd drawn dragons, symbols, and landscapes—all the sorts of things I loved to doodle—except she was *really* good. I was impressed.

I love dragons. . . . I like fantasy. . . . I like to draw, I said to myself in my head. I looked at the other two girls. One had boy-short brown hair and was wearing a blue-and-white-striped T-shirt and worn jeans. Her arms looked large and strong, and something about the way she held herself and spoke with confidence made me think she could handle herself in a fight against an entire group of boys. The other girl had long brown hair and the smoothest, most flawless skin I'd ever seen. She wore a black zip-up jacket and baggy jeans. All three of them had a sort of awkwardness to them that made me feel warm with familiarity. They reminded me of me.

"Oooh, I like the scales you did on that one," said the girl with long hair, leaning over.

"Thanks!" said the blond. "That one took me, like, three hours." She turned the page with her stubby fingers. "Hey, did you guys see the new *Naruto* episode?"

"It was awesome! I just wish they'd hurry up and catch up with the manga," said the girl with short hair.

"*Naruto*? I like *Naruto*!" I blurted out.

The three girls turned toward me with accusing stares, and I burned with humiliation. *So much for smoothly integrating into their group, Luke. Way to go, loser.*

But then the blond spoke. "Really? That's awesome. What episode are you on?"

"Um, I've seen all of them so far, but I haven't read any of the literature yet."

"You should! It's really good," said the short-haired girl. "I've already finished a few of the books. You could borrow them sometime if you'd like."

"I have them too," said the long-haired girl softly. I could tell she was the shyest of the three.

"Thanks!" I said.

"I'm Catherine," said the blond.

"Maria," said the short-haired girl.

"Lisa," said the shy girl.

"I'm Luke," I said just as the lunch bell rang.

"Come meet us for lunch tomorrow!" said Catherine.

"Yeah, I'll bring you my books," said Maria.

"Cool!" I said.

I went through the rest of the day with a spark of joy in my chest, knowing I had friends.

From then on our group was inseparable. Other kids, the jocks and cheerleader types, quickly saw me as a target, and pretty soon I was used to shouts of "fag" as I walked down the hall, along with the usual whispering and snickering whenever I walked into a room. I was able to tolerate it, though, because I knew I had Catherine, Maria, and Lisa. We ate lunch together, hung out at one another's houses after school, went to anime conventions, and talked for countless hours on the phone.

Like me, Maria also wrote her own fantasy book series, and the main characters were based on the four of us. We each represented one of the four elements. Catherine, with her spontaneous energy and potential to be as mean as hell, was fire. You never knew what Catherine was going to do next. Whenever anyone made fun of me, called me gay or a weirdo, Catherine would be ready to kick their ass, cuss them out, and throw stuff. She was literally a fireball.

Maria, short and husky, was earth. She loved animals and had no interest when Catherine and Lisa would talk about boys. I always wondered if she was a lesbian, but if so, she never came out. Like Catherine, Maria always defended me. When she wanted, she could be so intimidating, it was as if she were peering into your very being. "You don't know anything about Luke, so why don't you shut up and keep your thoughts to yourself," she'd say in an ice-cold voice. Even the confident jocks would freeze and lock down when they were up against Maria.

Lisa, quiet and nerdy with her long flowing hair, was wind. She was the most passive in our group, calm and reserved. I knew she cared about me, but she didn't have the guts to stick up for me the way Catherine and Maria did. Lisa and I mainly bonded over video games. She was obsessed with all the old vintage games.

I was water—the one who always went with the flow. I could be violent or I could be soft, gentle, and caring. When one of us was upset, I would be the one to counsel her; Catherine would be the one to say, "Let's all go skydiving!"; Maria would tell you to suck it up and shut up; and Lisa would just kind of sit in the back and be like, "Oh. . . . Mmmm."

Catherine and I grew especially close and were soon best friends. We clicked in that special way where we always knew how to make the other laugh. There was also something about her that made me trust her more than anyone else I knew. She was always open with her feelings, never hid anything, and seemed to genuinely want the best for other people. I wanted to confide in her about my confusions— how I felt wrong in my body and my attraction to boys—but I was scared. As open and warm as Catherine was, she came from a Catholic family that was staunchly homophobic. Whenever I went to her house, her mom or dad would be railing against some person who didn't fit into their idea of right and wrong, and they would talk about how that person was headed to hell. I decided it was better to keep my mouth shut. Of course, my true self slipped out in various ways all the time.

One time Catherine, Maria, Lisa, and I were all hanging out in Catherine's room, just lounging around, when Catherine asked Lisa to paint her fingernails. Catherine rooted through her Caboodles makeup kit and handed Lisa a sparkly blue color. I watched with envy as Lisa carefully slid the brush over each of Catherine's fingernails.

"Now toes!" said Catherine, kicking off her Vans.

"Ugh, your feet smell," said Maria, flipping through a Pokémon book.

"You're crazy. My feet smell like rose hips tea," said Catherine.

"What the hell is rose hips tea?" said Maria, and we all laughed.

Lisa stuck little cotton balls between Catherine's toes and got to work. Meanwhile Catherine fanned her fingers in the air and lightly blew on them. All of a sudden, I couldn't stand it anymore.

"Do me too!" I said.

"They can't do you. You're a boy!" said Maria.

"So what?" I said. "It doesn't matter. Just do it."

"Sure, why not," said Catherine.

After Lisa finished Catherine's toes, Catherine rifled through her Caboodles again. "Any color preference, Luke?"

"Um, the plum-colored one," I said.

I scooted over toward Catherine. She took my hands and delicately painted each nail a vibrant plum coat.

"You're so strange, Luke," said Maria. "You're strange but we love you."

One thing I especially liked about my group was that although boys came up on occasion, that wasn't really our thing. Lisa did have a boyfriend for a while, but they never even kissed. We were all much more into fantasy and anime than dating, so I didn't have to worry too much about the pressure to "like a girl"—a pressure that was otherwise ubiquitous. People were always asking if Catherine and I were dating, which of course just made us laugh.

"Ew!" we'd both say at the same time.

"We're like siblings," I'd explain.

The constant boy-girl drama was impossible to escape, though. Everyone at school always needed to know which boys liked which girls and vice versa and who had or had not "done stuff." We all clocked one another's development with roving eyes as well. All of our bodies were changing at a rapid pace. The boys sprouted up twenty feet over a long weekend, it seemed, while the girls showed up with filled-out bras.

For me puberty was nothing short of traumatizing. The first time I found a hair in my armpit, it sent me into a spiral of panic and I sobbed every night before bed for a week. All I wanted was to be a beautiful girl like the models I saw on billboards, but instead I had horrific visions of myself transforming into a brutish, muscled, hairy man. As much as I feared this, though, my puberty was clearly different from the other boys around me. My voice cracked, then evened out, but never became deep. I did grow hair in my under-arms and in my pubic area, but barely any on my face, and what was there was thin and soft. Most confusing, I began to develop small breasts. Of course, part of me loved this—I'd always wanted to grow boobs, and it felt like a small confirmation that I was really a girl. But at the same time, I wasn't a girl, and I knew growing breasts was not normal. I did know some boys who had developed breasts, but they were all overweight, while I was ninety pounds. I had a feminine face, breasts, and a penis—none of it made any sense. I was too embarrassed to tell anyone and was scared what people would think if they saw the little lumps poking out of my chest, so I wore a bulky black hoodie to hide my body, even on 110-degree blistering hot days.

As much as I tried to hide myself away, my femininity in physicality and behavior was apparent to everyone, and I was viewed—like in Okay—with suspicion and ridicule. I had my crew of Catherine, Maria, and Lisa, but pretty much everyone else thought I was a freak. Rumors about me abounded: that I was gay or that I was a girl in disguise. This one really popular girl named Skylar soon had all her minions calling me "Lucy." In class they'd say, "Hey, Lucy-I-mean-Luke—hee, hee, hee—can you pass me the stapler?" Like many bullies, they were disappointingly unoriginal.

Once, Maria tried calling me Lucy too.

"Fuck you. *Don't* call me that," I said.

"Damn, I'm sorry," she said. "It was just as a joke. . . . I won't do it again." She was genuinely surprised at how upset I got.

You might think I would have liked being called a girl's name, but I knew people were saying it to make fun of me, and it wasn't a name I had chosen. It was out of my control, so I hated it.

I seemed to veer violently back and forth between wanting to hide, to not be seen by anyone, and wanting to rebel and let my true self be known—society be damned. At the same time that I felt self-loathing, I also felt this driving force within me that I was special and unique and deserved to be on this planet just like everyone else. On occasion I snuck into the girls' bathroom at school. If I got caught, I'd just pretend to have been confused. I grew my hair out long and would get violent with my mom when she tried to cut it, throwing the scissors across the room. I grew my nails out, stole my mom's nail polish, and gave them a clear coat every day. I plucked my eyebrows and shaved my legs.

One time this kid named Neil transferred to our school and was really chatty with me during homeroom.

"Hey, can I copy your homework?" he asked.

"This is homeroom. There's no homework," I said, laughing.

"What class do you have next? Can I copy that homework?" he said, and flashed me a grin. He had light eyes and a spray of freckles. He was really cute.

"Why don't we just see if we actually have any more classes together," I said, "and then I'll consider it."

"I hope we do," he said.

Was he flirting with me?

Every time I glanced over at Neil during the rest of homeroom, he was sitting there smiling at me. I didn't have any more classes with him the rest of the day, but the next morning I could feel my heart thumping as I walked into homeroom, looking for him. He was standing with a clump of boys.

"Hey, Neil," I said.

Neil looked at me and then quickly looked away. He didn't even say hi back. Totally confused and ashamed, I sat down and opened my school binder. I tried to pretend to be absorbed in my homework, but my cheeks were burning. What had just happened?

That day at lunch I told Catherine about it.

"He just ignored me, like we hadn't had this whole conversation yesterday."

Catherine had a weird expression on her face.

"What? Tell me," I said.

"Neil Pears? The new kid?"

"Yeah."

"He thought you were a girl."

"W-what?"

"Kirsten told me that he told Jonathan Brewer he liked you, and Jonathan was like, 'Dude, that's Luke—he's a boy.' I guess Neil got really embarrassed."

I felt a weird mixture of embarrassment myself, but also a thrill. *I am a girl,* I screamed inside my head.

"So now Neil says he's gonna kick your ass, but forget that—you know I won't let anyone touch you," continued Catherine.

Whatever thrill I'd had now disappeared and was replaced by familiar anxiety.

Meanwhile, on top of my troubles at school, life at home was miserable. My dad and I were two cold strangers. Jake had become spoiled and petulant, constantly playing Mom and Dad off each other in order to get what he wanted. My parents barely spoke to each other anymore, and if they did, it was her telling him he needed to quit drinking and him telling her to leave him alone. My mom had grown up with an alcoholic father, and she just couldn't do that to her kids anymore. Finally she told my dad she wanted a divorce.

I'd seen plenty of movies where parents sit their kids down and as kindly as possible explain to them that the separation *isn't their fault* but Mom and Dad won't be living together anymore. Then the kids ask questions, maybe cry, and the parents try to console them. This is not how the divorce went down in our family. Rather than our parents actually telling us, the divorce just started happening. My mom told Jake and me she was looking for a new house for us. One night I was watching TV, and I overheard my mom and dad in the kitchen.

"You're gonna regret this. You'll never make it without me," my dad said. His voice was cold and slurred.

"I don't need your money. I don't need anything. I just need to protect my children," she said.

I turned the sound down to try to hear more, but they had stopped. My dad left the kitchen and went upstairs to his den.

I knew my parents' marriage had been troubled for years, so when the divorce started happening, it didn't really surprise me. Jake and I never spoke of it—we just didn't have that kind of relationship. I heard him complaining to Mom that there wasn't going to be enough money left, which was maybe the only way he knew to express distress. I didn't really talk to Catherine, Maria, or Lisa about it either. In a way, I think I was embarrassed, and I didn't want to burden them with my problems.

One day at lunch I just announced, "Oh, my parents are getting divorced."

"Really?" said Catherine. "Are you okay?"

"Oh my God," said Maria.

"It's fine. Hey, you guys want to go to the comic book shop after school? I want to get some more Pokémon books."

"Uh . . . sure," said Catherine. "You're sure you don't want to talk about your parents?"

"Seriously, it's fine," I said. "So . . . comic shop?"

"I'm up for the comic shop," said Maria.

I was the one they came to for emotional support, and reversing those roles made me uncomfortable. I think in some ways my being the only "boy" in the group had landed me this role as counselor. Also, I didn't really see the point in going into the subject of the divorce. My parents were getting divorced. I was moving. It sucked. What else was there to say?

I turned thirteen right around the time when the divorce started. The previous year's joyous pool party in Okay, with Dad flipping burgers and Mom singing karaoke, seemed as though it were from another lifetime. Unlike the memory of that party, which feels crisp and bright, my memory of turning thirteen is blurry and dark, as if it were almost more dream than reality.

My birthday fell on a Saturday, and I slept in late. When I woke up, I got dressed in my usual uniform: baggy jeans; a black T-shirt with one of those sayings like I GOT OUT OF BED FOR THIS?; and of course my large black sweatshirt, hood pulled over my greasy, uncombed hair. My mom was planning to move Jake and me out of the house any day, so all my stuff was packed up in boxes, giving my bedroom an abandoned feeling.

I walked downstairs, where Jake had the TV blaring, watching *SpongeBob SquarePants*. My mom had bought a chocolate cake, and it sat on the kitchen counter. In a rare instance of family togetherness, my mom, Dad, and Jake all gathered to eat breakfast together and to watch me blow out my candles. I wished what I always wished, what I wished for whenever the clock was 11:11, and what I prayed for at night in bed. As impractical and absurd as it seemed, I wished to wake up the next day as a beautiful woman.

Mom, Dad, and Jake each gave me fifty dollars. (Though the fifty from Jake was really from Mom and Dad.) I was a practical child and figured, *Why not save everyone the time and effort of finding me a present I probably wouldn't even like, and just receive money and buy what I want?*

"Do you want to invite Catherine, Maria, and Lisa over?" my mom asked. "I could take you guys to a movie."

"No," I said. The truth was, I felt too depressed to see them. Turning thirteen especially scared me because I was now officially a teenager—my descent into manhood would only get worse. Just as I hadn't wanted to talk to Catherine, Maria, or Lisa about the divorce, I also didn't want them to see me so down on my birthday. I didn't like showing my emotions around people—it made me feel weak and vulnerable. Also, I'd had such terrible experiences with therapists, I figured, *Well, if a therapist can't help me, there's no way a thirteen-year-old girl can.*

"You're sure? They could come over for dinner. Or just Catherine."

"She's busy. She's got family stuff," I lied.

Instead I had my mom drive me to Walmart, where I used my birthday money to buy *King Kong* for my PlayStation 2. When we got home, I shut myself away in my room and played it for the rest of the day. By the time night fell, I had forgotten it was my birthday.

. . .

In the fall of 2008, I began high school at Bixby High. Catherine, Maria, Lisa, and I were still best friends, and I treasured them—especially Catherine—but my depression had only become worse. Every day the pressure of being not just a boy but soon a *man* weighed more heavily on me. Existence felt unbearable. My mom had moved Jake and me to a small house on the other side of Bixby, and I spent most nights stewing in my pain in my ten-by-ten bedroom.

It got to the point where on some days I hated every face I saw. I couldn't even stomach the sound of other people's voices. I hated them so much for being human and normal, while I was stuck with this curse. I wanted them to feel my pain so badly, and I wanted to walk in their shoes for eternity. I would excuse myself from class almost every day because I just needed to go outside and be alone.

Being a teenager, hormones churned inside me, and I felt plagued by sexual urges. I thought about sex constantly but rarely masturbated—partially because of my Christian mindset that masturbation was a sin, and partially because I hated my body. Also, I liked the strong feeling that abstaining from masturbating gave me. It made me feel in control of my body to not succumb to the urges. I even wore a purity ring—a ring to symbolize that I was saving myself for marriage—for a few years. The Jonas Brothers were popular, and they wore purity rings, so it seemed like the thing to do. Purity ring or not, though, I couldn't stop feeling guilty and anxious over my various "sinful" thoughts and feelings—not just my sexual urges but also my gender confusion. Sometimes I tried bargaining with God, telling him I would go to church every weekend and become fundamentally devout if only he would cure me of sin and make me feel normal. But of course, no matter how many times I wished, prayed, or even pretended to summon magical powers from the spirit world, nothing changed. I wondered if God were punishing me for being bad in a past life, or if my parents had been sinners. Maybe he simply wanted to laugh at me and was just as evil as everyone else. By the time I turned fourteen, I decided I'd had enough of God. I was sick of bargaining, sick of living in fear, and sick of believing in someone or something that apparently hated me. I became an atheist.

It was also around this time that I started turning to Google for answers. I began with trepidation, typing in phrases such as "How to know if you're gay" or "I'm gay but don't feel gay." This usually led to information on drag queens—something I knew for certain I wasn't. Eventually I worked up the courage to, with apprehension, actually type the phrase, "I feel like I'm a girl trapped in a boy's body," but this was no better. It was the same old drag queen and cross-dresser links.

It may seem crazy to you that nothing about being transgender popped up—but in 2008, as far as I could find, it just didn't. I admittedly didn't search too hard. Often I'd sit down at the computer and quickly type, "I'm a boy but feel like a girl," and if nothing that resonated popped up immediately, I'd erase my search history and quickly sign off. I felt guilty and anxious for searching at all. I think that for years, even though deep down I knew I was a girl, some part of me was still holding on to somehow becoming that "perfect" straight boy my parents and society wanted.

Then, one cold night in January when I was fifteen, it happened. My mom was putting Jake to bed, and I went into the computer room to try searching for answers one more time. I sat down and typed the usual, "I feel like I'm a girl trapped in a boy's body," and this time I was greeted with something new.

It was an article called *"I'm a Girl"—Understanding Transgender Children*.

And that was it. That was the first time I ever read the magic word: "transgender."

I sat in front of the computer, my heart racing, as I read about Jazz Jennings, a six-year-old girl who had been born a boy. The article said that as soon as he could speak, Jazz made it clear he wanted to wear girl clothes. When his parents told Jazz he was a "good boy," he would correct them and say, "You mean 'good girl.'" At first Jazz's parents were confused and scared, but Jazz kept insisting his penis was a mistake. Slowly they began to accept Jazz. They allowed her to wear a girl bathing suit at her fifth birthday, then girl clothes in public, and then, when she turned six, she began kindergarten as a girl. Jazz's parents were wholly supportive. They just wanted to do whatever was necessary to keep their child happy, healthy, and safe.

As I read, I realized tears of joy were streaming down my face. There *was* someone like me. I was *not* alone.

The article on Jazz led me to links on other transgender stories, and I learned that there were actually thousands of transgenders out there. I read about hormone replacement therapies and surgeries, people who had actually managed to transition from one gender to the other. I searched for videos and found one where Oprah interviews an African-American woman in her twenties who had transitioned from male to female. Everything the woman said resonated with me. She talked about always feeling like a girl inside and how when she used to imagine her wedding, she would always be wearing a dress. She said she never once regretted her decision to transition.

I couldn't believe it. All this time, there was actually something I could do.

It was around ten p.m., and my mom had finished putting Jake to sleep. I walked back into my room, lay on my bed, curled up in the fetal position, and rocked back and forth, crying heavily.

Knock, knock.

"What?" I said.

My mom gingerly cracked the door open. "Luke, honey? What's wrong?"

My mom was constantly asking me what was wrong, to the point where it had stopped having meaning. That was her daily existence, living with a chronically depressed child. This time, however, I had something to say. I sat up, my cheeks soaked with tears, and she came over and sat down on the bed next to me. I looked her straight in the eyes.

"Every time I've tried to talk to you about my confusion, the only answer has been 'You'll be fine,' or therapy or medications. But I need you to really listen to me."

My mom's eyes welled up. In a soft voice she said, "Okay. . . ."

I started talking, and soon it felt like I couldn't stop. Every thought, every feeling, every confusion I'd been having for the past decade poured out of me.

"I feel like a freak. Everyone at school thinks I'm a freak. They call me 'fag' and whisper about me. Catherine and Maria stand up for me, but it doesn't matter. Every day is the same, and it feels like hell."

"I'll talk to the school—" my mom started to say.

"No. Just listen," I interrupted. "I'm miserable at home, too. I feel like you and Dad favor Jake because he's normal, because he acts the way a boy is supposed to. I don't think Dad even loves me anymore. It makes me feel hopeless, like I have no purpose. I've thought about killing myself."

My mom started to cry. "Every day when I come home from work, that's what I fear," she said. "That this will be the day I find you dead."

I wrapped my arms tight around my knees and stared at the ground. "I've just felt like there's something wrong with me for so long," I said.

"Luke," she said. "It's okay if you're gay. I don't care."

"I'm not gay," I said, looking up. "I'm transgender."

My mom looked utterly confused.

"You mean like in *The Rocky Horror Picture Show*?" she said. "That man who dresses up with makeup?"

"No. That's a transvestite. I'm transgender. I'm a girl with a boy's body, and I want to change that."

Her face shifted from confusion to dark disappointment. "Transgender?" She said it as if it were an evil word.

"Can't you just be gay?" She began to cry again.

It was painful to hear her reject the word "transgender," to want to shove aside the one thing I knew was right. But there was no going back now. I persevered and took her hand. "Let me show you," I said.

We went into the computer room, where I showed her the article about Jazz. I watched her face as she read, and I knew she was having the same reaction I'd had. Jazz sounded exactly like me.

"She's even obsessed with *The Little Mermaid*, just like you were," said my mom.

"I know!"

I directed my mom to the Oprah interview and more transgender articles. She sat there, reading every word carefully, taking it all in. After a while she turned to me.

"Will this make you happy, baby?"

I felt a rush of overwhelming relief. "Yes," I said. "I think it will. I just want to be a girl."

"Okay," my mom said softly, and she put her arms around me.

We sat there and hugged each other tight, both bawling.

My mom wiped her eyes, straightened, and held on to my shoulders. "Then we are going to do this. Make me a list of everything you want done, and I will make sure I do every single thing on it."

"Really?" I said.

"You just have to promise me one thing."

"What?" I said, wiping my nose.

"You cannot kill yourself. I can't help you, I can't fix this, if you kill yourself. You have got to promise me that no matter how hard it gets, you will not take your life."

I looked at my mom, her green eyes wet and bloodshot from crying. "I promise," I said.

"Okay. You hold your promise. I swear I'll hold mine."

This is the list I gave my mom:

- Go by "she," not "he"

- Get rid of boy clothes and buy girl clothes

- Find a support group and meet people like me

- Start hormones

- Legally change my name

- Go to school as a girl

- Change my name and sex on all ID cards and birth certificate

- Get genital reconstruction surgery

And she stayed true to her word. My mom did everything she could to help me tick each item off. First I thought about what I wanted my new name to be. I briefly considered "Fay," which I liked the sound of, but I realized kids at school could rhyme "Fay" with "gay," so I nixed that. I'd also always loved the name Katie—I thought it sounded mellow and home-on-the-prairie-ish. It felt like me. It felt like who I wanted to be. I chose "Katie" for my first name and "Rain" for my middle name, based on my Rainfall series. As soon as I told my mom my decision, she began referring to me as Katie and "she." She slipped up a lot at first, but I knew she was trying.

Additionally, my mom started putting a little money aside each week so that we could get new clothes for me. And she immediately started looking for a support group. A friend of hers told her about Openarms Youth Project (OYP) in Tulsa, which had support groups for LGBT teens. She asked if I wanted to try it out, and I said, "When's the soonest we can go?" On the drive over I was so excited imagining all the other transgenders I would meet and how they would help me find my confidence. I still looked how I always had—pale, sickly skin, greasy hair hidden under my giant black hoodie, braces and glasses, baggy jeans. But I was ready to tell people who I really was. We parked in the lot outside the modest, tan brick building, and I took a deep breath.

We went inside and met Ken and Tim, a gay couple who own OYP and were running the meeting. They both looked to be in their late thirties or early forties. Ken had cool teal-colored glasses.

"Welcome!" Ken said. "And you are?"

"Katie Rain Hill," I said. It was the first time I'd ever introduced myself with my new name.

"It's great to meet you, Katie," Tim said.

"I'll be back in an hour," my mom said.

I sat down in the circle of chairs, along with about ten other teens.

"Okay. We're going to go around the circle, and I want everyone to say your name and whether you're a vampire or a werewolf."

"I'm Andrea," said a large girl in a tie-dyed shirt with a bleached-blond strip in her hair. "I'm a werewolf. And a lesbian," she added.

Everyone chuckled.

"I'm Jeanie," said a soft-spoken black girl. "Werewolf."

"Trina," said a white girl with a shaved head. "Vampire."

"What's up. I'm Brendan, vampire," said a boy with gorgeous black hair and piercing blue eyes. I instantly developed a crush on him. *Yeah, but he's probably gay. That's why he's here,* I thought. *Unless maybe he's bi? Please be bi. Please be bi.*

"I'm Robbie, werewolf," said a thin boy with wispy brown hair. He leaned his head onto Brendan's shoulder.

Great. They're probably dating. It was my turn.

"I'm Katie. Vampire, I guess," I said.

"Katie?" said Andrea, obviously confused because I still looked like a boy.

"Yeah, I'm transgender," I said.

"What's that?" asked Brendan.

"It's like you feel like you're trapped in the wrong gender . . . right?" asked Ken, looking at me.

I felt kind of anxious. Ken was the group leader—shouldn't he have known for certain what transgender was? Why had he phrased it like a question?

"Yeah," I said. "I'm a girl in a boy's body. I like guys, but I want them to see me as a girl."

"Cool," said Tim. "You're actually our first transgender in a long time."

"Like . . . ten years?" asked Ken.

Tim nodded.

"I still don't get it," said Brendan.

"It kind of sounds like you're just gay," said Andrea.

"I'm not. I'm transgender."

"Yeah, it sounds like you're gay but you like dressing up in women's clothes," a boy with curly gelled hair and acne said.

"You seem gay to me," Robbie offered.

It was incredibly frustrating, but the thing was, even though these kids didn't understand, they weren't rude about it. They were all willing to sit and listen as I tried to explain. And then Jeanie said:

"This is really cool. I've never met a transgender person before."

Everyone started nodding and agreeing at the same time.

"Totally cool," said Andrea.

When the group was over, I told my mom I wanted to keep coming back. After a few weeks I considered OYP my family.

Even though I had a support group, my mom also insisted that I start therapy again. The last time I'd been to a therapist had been when I was eleven. He was a psychiatrist I saw twice who prescribed an antidepressant that didn't work. After him my mom promised we could finally stop with all the therapists and medications. But now she wanted me to go again, and I was wary.

"This is a big deal, this transgender thing," she told me. "I want you to talk to a professional."

I begrudgingly agreed, and a few days later we drove to a large glass building that housed many offices. I was dressed as Katie in girl clothes but felt incredibly self-conscious and socially awkward.

"Does she know about me?" I asked my mom as we sat in the waiting room.

"Yes, I spoke with her on the phone and told her what you're going through right now."

The thought of the two of them talking about me made me cringe.

"Katie?" a woman with long brown hair in her thirties said, opening the door to the inner office.

"Uh, yeah," I said. I got up and followed her inside.

It was a cold, clinical office, with an uncomfortable, hard couch. The therapist sat down in a chair across from me. She seemed to be observing me from a distance rather than looking forward to getting to know me.

"So," she said, "tell me about yourself. What do you like to do? Who are your friends? What subjects do you like?"

She rattled off questions as if I were in an interview. The last thing I felt like doing was answering them. I made a halfhearted attempt.

"I like staying alone in my room," I said.

The therapist frowned as if I were playing with her, which I wasn't. I was just being honest.

"I heard you've been experiencing bullying. Can you tell me what the kids at school say?"

Why does it matter exactly what they say? I thought. *They make my life hell and there's nothing I can do about it. Case closed.*

"I don't know," I said.

Our session continued with more of the same—her asking questions in her cold, matter-of-fact voice, and me giving brief, curt answers.

"Well, we certainly have a lot more to cover," she said when our hour was up. The way she said it, it sounded as if I had somehow failed our therapy session.

Can't wait, I thought.

As my mom and I drove home from the therapist's office, I turned to her.

"Mom, I really didn't like her. Can I please not go back?"

My mom sighed. "If you really don't think she can help you, then I suppose you don't have to go back."

"Thank you," I said. Ever since I'd come out as trans, my mom had really begun to listen to me.

We were silent for a while as she drove.

"Luke—I mean Katie," my mom said. "We need to let your dad know."

"I couldn't care less whether he knows or not," I replied, staring straight ahead.

My dad and I had barely spoken in five years. When my mom divorced him, he removed me from his will, leaving everything to Jake. He told my mom, "Luke doesn't care about me, and I don't care about him." Mom hadn't been planning on telling me that, but Dad told Jake, and of course the first thing Jake did was run to me, saying, "Ha-ha! All

of Dad's money is going to me, and you're getting nothing!"
I knew my dad expected me to go to him and tell him I
wanted a relationship again. But I refused. The way I saw
it, it was the parent's job to reach out to the child. Since
my mom, Jake, and I had moved, I'd been back to my dad's
house maybe twice.

I wasn't going to come out to him, but my mom insisted
he know, so when the two of them were alone, she sat him
down and told him I was transgender. As she told me later,
it did not go well.

"He's telling you he's a *what*? No. I won't have a freak
for a son," he apparently said.

My mom tried to explain what "transgender" meant, but
at this point her only information had come from the few
articles I had shown her. She still didn't really understand
transgenderism herself. As she put it to me later, "All I really
knew was that it was worse than being gay." Thankfully, my
mother has come a long way since then in her understanding
of the LGBT community. But at the time, my parents' only
experience of gay was sadly not a good one. Right around
when I came out as trans, my father's brother, Larry, who
had come out as gay in his late thirties, died from AIDS.

Larry's coming out had shocked my father. His brother
had always been the super-masculine one, rugged and tough.
If anything, my dad had been the feminine one. Sure, he was
a hard-as-nails marine, but he also had some delicate characteristics. My mom told me that when I was a small child, she
didn't really question my girlish habits of always crossing
my legs or flitting my hands, because Dad did those things
too. And they didn't make him any less of the straight man

he was. So Dad was surprised when Larry came out, but unlike his sisters, Shauna and Leslie, who were still devout Mormons and cut Larry off, my dad accepted it. Larry had been living with a man for ten years when they found out they were both HIV positive. When my mom told Dad that I was trans, he said he was scared I was going to get AIDS too.

"We don't know that," she said. "We'll deal with it if that happens, but we don't know that it will."

Despite his initial repulsion, my dad did ultimately accept my being trans. But it didn't exactly help our relationship either. We never *really* talked about it, and the alienation between us grew wider.

The same day my mom told my dad, she also told Jake as well as her entire extended family.

Jake was ten at the time, and he and I were still not close. As with my dad, I told my mom I didn't want to tell Jake but that she could. She told me later how it went, which, as with my dad, was not great. She said he was confused and mainly concerned with how it would affect him. He didn't know how to explain to people that his brother was now his sister, and he was worried he would be made fun of. My mom told him, "You've always had a sister. We just didn't know. You can tell your friends that Luke is female on the inside but was born with male parts, and it wasn't until he was older that we found out. Now he needs to undergo surgery so he can be what he wants to be, which is a girl. We raised her the wrong way. It's not her fault or your fault; it's Mom and Dad's fault." I guess my brother accepted that as an answer. He and I never had a conversation about my transition, though. He just tentatively began to call me Katie, and shortly after, "Sis."

Mom's extended family have a zero-tolerance policy for anything "gay." She knew the conversation would not go over well, but in a way that made it easier. She knew she could leave no room for pushback. She told my dad and Jake in the morning and then called her mom, brother, and sister and told them to meet at their mom's house because she had something important to tell them. She then drove two hours down to Wagoner, sat them all down, and simply said, "Luke is now Katie. She's transgender, and I'm standing by my child. Everyone needs to learn to start calling him 'she,' and if anyone has a problem with that, I will never see any of you again." It worked. The next time the whole family got together, everyone made an effort to accept me.

Despite my mom's insistence that the family accept me, the truth was, as she told me later, she was still having trouble accepting it herself. Though she was putting up a good front, she's since told me that in the beginning few weeks, she was terrified and would sob by herself in her bedroom when she knew I couldn't hear. Living in Oklahoma, she was worried how others would react. She told me she imagined me walking around in garish makeup and trashy women's clothes and getting jumped, possibly murdered. She imagined someone burning our house down.

In addition to the fear and confusion, both of my parents also had to mourn the loss of Luke. I hated Luke and was happy to see him go, but Luke had been their son, the little boy they had given birth to and raised. Acknowledging that he no longer existed was painful. Right after I came out,

I asked my mom to take down all the photos in the house of me as a boy (except for one from Japan, where I'm three and wearing a kimono). She did as I requested but asked if she could at least keep the photos in her scrapbooks.

"No, throw them out. I never want to look at them again," I said. I'd been Katie for only a matter of days but was ready to completely excise Luke from my life.

I flipped through my mom's scrapbooks often and did not ever again want to look at photos of me as a bald-headed baby propped up next to basketballs and footballs at a photography studio, or images of me as a little boy riding my bike, surrounded by cutout drawings of cars and the words "Boy Stuff."

"How about I just keep the scrapbooks in the attic for a while," my mom said. "You never have to look at them, but if you ever want to, when you're older, they'll be there."

"Fine," I said.

One night a few weeks after I first came out to her, my mom asked if I'd like her to do my makeup. I almost started crying with joy. We went into her huge walk-in closet with its glittery chandelier, rows of gorgeous dresses on hangers, and bureaus heaped with jewelry and accessories. She unhooked one of her most expensive dresses—a snow-white ball gown with a fur-rimmed neck. I changed into the dress, and then she sat me down and applied my makeup. As I felt the base go on, then the blush, then the familiar lip gloss, I could easily say that at that point it was the happiest day of my life.

"I can't believe how much you look like a girl!" my mom

said, stepping back with a huge smile. "You're beautiful! I don't know how I managed to miss this before." She ran to get her camera and take pictures.

When I looked at myself in the mirror, though, I did not have the same reaction. I thought I looked hideous. Just an awkward boy wearing too much makeup and an ill-fitting dress. It killed me that I was going to have to work so hard just to appear to others as an ugly girl, while other girls got to be beautiful without even trying. Still, I couldn't give up.

But my mom loved the photos. One night a few weeks later, she came into my room and said she had something to show me. She'd taken a scrapbook down from the attic and had added the new photos along with all the rest. There was now a page with me in the white dress and a tiara and with a nervous smile, surrounded by cutout images of a purse and high heels and the words "Big Sister."

I knew I had to tell Catherine, Maria, and Lisa, but I didn't know how. There was also an added complication. For the past year I had been lying to them that I had a twin sister, not coincidentally named Katie. Just as I had expertly manipulated Dr. Ashman into thinking I was a sports-loving, all-American boy when I was eight, I had skillfully deceived my best friends. I'd told them Katie was a fashion model who lived in New York City with my aunt and her best friend, Terry, a twenty-three-year-old lesbian. I'd basically given Katie my fantasy life. I'd told them that Terry the lesbian was a little crazy and spontaneous and had an obsession with apples. As I've said before, the key to a good lie is in the details. Details, details, details,

details. I had a friend from Florida, Perry, who had come out as gay, and I'd told them that he hung out with Terry and Katie too. I researched fashion shows in New York online so that if anyone asked me, I could say Katie was at this show on this date at this time, with facts to back it up.

At first I made up my twin sister as a way to express my emotions. Catherine and Lisa and some other girls would be talking about the Jonas Brothers (don't judge—we all thought they were cute!), and I'd be able to say, "Oh my God, my twin sister *loves* Nick Jonas. She thinks he's so hot." And they'd fold me into the conversation.

"Yeah, Nick's hot, but Joe's hotter."

"What about Robert Pattinson? Now, that's a hottie."

"What!" I'd say. "My twin sister thinks Robert Pattinson is stupid. She thinks he's ugly."

"Well, your twin sister is stupid."

"No, she's not! Come on. If you think about it, he looks dirty. . . ."

I could talk and share my opinions without them thinking I was gay or weird. Eventually the whole school thought I had a twin sister.

One day as I troubled over how to tell my friends I was trans, it hit me—I didn't have to. I would simply say I was going away to study in another country, and my twin sister Katie was moving here. It seemed like a brilliant, perfect plan, and I began to slowly, carefully put it into effect. One night I was on the phone with Maria, telling her how I was going to have to move but she would get to meet my twin sister, when my mom overheard me. She was standing outside my door when I hung up the phone.

"Who is this twin sister?" my mom said.

I froze for a moment. "Mom, I need you to do this for me."

"Do what?"

"Everyone thinks I have a twin sister who's a model and lives with your sister in New York."

"My sister lives in Fort Gibson."

"No, she lives in New York, and if anyone asks, you have to tell them, yes, I have a twin sister, and she's moving here."

"Oh, good Lord."

"Mom, please! I can't tell them I'm trans. I have to do it this way."

My mom agreed, and when anyone asked, she confirmed that Katie lived in New York but was moving back home soon. My mom had taken a photo of me wearing hair extensions and a fancy belly dancing costume from Dubai. It was one of the few photos of myself that I liked. When my friends came over, I'd show it to them and say, "Doesn't my twin sister, Katie, look great?"

As clever as it all was, I ached to let my friends know the truth, especially Catherine. It had felt so good to tell my mom, and I wanted to explain to Catherine who I really was and know that she still loved and accepted me too. I was scared, though, mostly because Catherine's family were devout Catholics. If I told her, she might hate me. I had to go through with it, though, so with a swelling feeling in my chest, I curled up on my bed and dialed her number.

"Hi, Luke!"

"Hey!"

"What's up?"

"Nothing. . . ."

"Cool. I have so much homework. What are you doing?"

"Nothing. . . . Uh, look, I have something to tell you."

"Are you okay? You sound weird."

Just do it. Just tell her. It will be okay.

"I'm not a boy; I'm a girl. It's called transgender. I've been reading about it on the Internet, and it's a real thing. I want to transition into being a girl."

I held my breath as I listened to the silence on the other end of the phone. *"That's disgusting! You're going to hell!"* I imagined her saying. But then, after about twenty seconds, Catherine spoke.

"Oh. Well. Um. Okay," she said.

"Is that okay?" I asked.

"Yeah. Oh, that reminds me. I saw the *cutest* boy in band class the other day. I think you would really like him. He's so pretty. He's got these gorgeous eyes—"

"Is he straight?"

"Yeah."

"So . . . he probably wouldn't like me, then."

"Why wouldn't he? You're a girl; he's a boy. What's the problem?"

A giant grin spread across my face. Even though Catherine was hard-core Christian, and her family wouldn't approve, and she wasn't LGBT herself or judged in any similar way, she immediately grasped my situation better than anyone else had.

"I mean, I've always kind of suspected it," she said. "I

thought you were gay, but this makes sense too. I get it. It's not your fault. I still love you. You're still the same Luke."

A couple of weeks later I told her I wanted to be called Katie.

"But isn't that your twin sister's name?" she asked.

"Um, I am my twin sister."

Catherine just laughed and laughed.

I wasn't ready to go out in public as Katie yet, but I began to dress as a girl to go to my weekly support group meetings at OYP and to their Saturday night dances. With the money we had saved, my mom took me shopping and helped me pick out girl clothes we could afford.

"What do you want me to do with all these old boy clothes?" she asked.

"Burn 'em, bury 'em, give 'em away. I don't care."

We actually had a ceremonial burning of some of my most hated items—the baggy sweaters I used to wear to hide my body. There were so many bad memories imprinted on them, I didn't want to give them away and risk passing on my misery to some poor bloke. All my boy's underwear went into the trash. From then on I wore panties and sometimes bras, which felt much more relaxing and comfortable. My mom bought me silicone pads to put into the bras to resemble breasts. I still had very small boobs that had developed naturally, but I wanted something more. She brought home makeup that was on discount at Food Pyramid, the supermarket where she worked in the pharmacy, and taught me how to apply it. Through trial and error I developed my own methods of application. I continued to grow my hair out, and my mom helped me decide how to style it. She printed out lists of foods I could eat that would make my eyes whiter, my hair shinier and less frizzy. She bought shampoo that would help my hair grow fast, and lotion for me to use after I shaved my legs and arms.

I went to OYP each week in a new girl outfit or with new earrings. Brendan, Andrea, Jeanie, Robbie, and the rest of the gang would compliment me and tell me how pretty I looked. It felt amazing. The only praise I had ever received before had been for my grades. It felt like I was actually being seen. (And by a hot guy like Brendan, no less! Who, by the way, was—sadly, for me—just gay, not bi.)

Catherine and I had been planning for months to go the Jonas Brothers concert when they came to Tulsa. When the night finally arrived, I decided this was going to be the first time I went out in public as Katie. A complication, though, was that we were going with Catherine's parents. I didn't want them to know, so I would have to be in a kind of in-between stage. And an in-between stage it was. Truth be told, I looked terrible. I didn't put on any makeup, I had my glasses, and I was wearing this giant hideous shirt with stars on it and my bra underneath. Still, it felt good to be there as a girl instead of a boy. Catherine called me Luke in front of her parents, but whenever we were apart from them, she called me Katie.

The Bank of Oklahoma Center was enormous, and Catherine and I jumped up and down in our bleacher seats, screaming along with everyone else as the flashing colorful lights began and the brothers took the stage. They opened with their hit "Paranoid," and Catherine screamed "Joe!" while I screamed "Nick!" Every now and then, though, I could see her parents staring at me, and I knew they were thinking, *What the crap?*

As I started my sophomore year of high school, I began to gradually, tentatively transition at school. I was still Luke, officially a boy, but I replaced my glasses with contacts, styled my hair like a girl's, and wore form-fitting jeans and my bra with silicone pads (albeit hidden under a baggy shirt and jacket). There had always been rumors about me, but now they intensified. People whispered that I wore a bra (true), that I had boobs (true), and that I was HIV positive (not true). I started to wear a little bit of makeup, regardless of comments such as "Gay!" and "Freak!" as I walked down the hall. I tried speaking with a school administrator to see if they could do anything to help me.

"Yes, Luke. Come in," Ms. Katz said. Ms. Katz wore heavy makeup and had her hair pulled back into a tight, shiny ponytail.

I walked into her office. There were drawings from kids and letters of thanks plastered all over her walls.

"Hey," I said. "Um, the kids keep teasing. Calling me names and stuff."

Ms. Katz eyed me warily. I think she was trying to tell whether I was wearing makeup or not. I'd put on a very slight amount of foundation that morning.

"Who specifically?" she said.

"Football players mainly. Carter and some of the other guys. And some girls. Skylar."

Ms. Katz nodded and jotted down some notes. "We'll take care of it," she said.

But the next day Carter was back to pushing me in the halls. Skylar was back to whispering "Lucy" when I was called on in class. Nothing had changed. I went back to Ms. Katz a second time, and she reassured me they'd take care of it. The day after that the teasing was even worse.

"*Snitch,*" Skylar sneered at me in the hall.

"Don't get too close. It will give you AIDS," a football player called out.

I went back to Ms. Katz a third time.

"What is it, Luke?" Ms. Katz said, sighing loudly as I walked into the room.

"The teasing is worse—" I started to say, but Ms. Katz interrupted me.

"Well, maybe you shouldn't be such a tattletale," she said. "Besides, boys will be boys. There's not all that much I can do. You're just going to have to get used to it."

I couldn't believe it. This was a school official saying this to me. What else was I supposed to do besides come to her?

"Okay. Well, never mind, then," I said, and I walked out of her room. I never went back to the school for help again.

Meanwhile, I got up the courage to come out to Maria and Lisa. Catherine had kept my secret, but it felt weird keeping my other two closest friends in the dark. One day at lunch, while Catherine was there to support me, I did it.

"So . . . I have something to tell you guys," I said. I glanced over at Catherine, and she smiled encouragingly. "I'm trans. I'm, like, a girl. I go by the name Katie now."

"I thought your twin sister was Katie?" said Maria. She

looked between Catherine and me, her body tense.

"No, I'm Katie. . . ."

"Isn't that funny?" said Catherine.

"Not really," said Maria. "And I don't get it. What do you mean you're a girl?"

"It's called transgender, when you're born into the wrong body. There are a lot of people like me. . . ."

Lisa was just staring at me, her mouth sealed shut.

"I know it's a lot to take in," I said. "I just . . . I wanted to be open with you."

"And you knew?" said Maria, looking at Catherine.

Catherine nodded.

"Okay . . . ," said Maria. "I mean, I don't totally get it . . . but if that's what you say you are . . . I guess that's okay."

I looked at Lisa.

"Yeah, okay," said Lisa softly.

The next day, however, nothing was cool. When we all met for lunch, Lisa and Maria had stony looks on their faces.

"I can't do it," said Maria. "I can't be friends with a freak. My family thinks you're going to turn me into a lesbian, and I'm not a lesbian."

You might be, I thought.

"That's silly," I said, trying to make light of it. But Maria's expression stayed cold.

"My mom said you're the devil's spawn and are going to turn me into a lesbian and drag me to hell," said Lisa in her quiet voice.

"Katie is *not* the devil's spawn," said Catherine. "They're just crazy."

"Do *you* guys think I am?" I asked Maria and Lisa.

"I just can't do this," said Maria.

Then Maria and Lisa picked up their lunch trays and walked away from the table.

"Hey, are you okay?" Catherine asked.

I looked down at my tray of lasagna and mushy peas. "I'm not hungry," I said. "I think I'm just gonna go to lab science early." I picked up my tray to leave.

"Comic book shop after school?" said Catherine.

"Sure," I said with a weak smile.

It's okay, I told myself. *You still have Catherine.*

But about a week later Catherine's parents found out. I arrived at school to find Catherine crying by her locker.

"They told me, 'If you keep hanging out with that boy, you deserve to be stoned to death.'"

"What? Your parents actually said that?" I couldn't believe parents would rather their daughter die than continue to hang out with me. But that was how they felt. By the end of the week, Catherine's parents had pulled her out of every class we had together. They'd even gone to the school to demand that Catherine and I never be in each other's vicinity, including during lunch and recess. If teachers ever spotted Catherine and me together, they were to report it to Catherine's parents immediately.

Since they couldn't demand that Catherine never be near me just because they didn't like me, they made up a lie that I was threatening Catherine's life. They told the school I was cornering Catherine, saying, "I'm gonna kill you," and things like that. This led to even more complications, because the school then started an investigation to expel me. My dad, who was a teacher at Bixby High, running the marine ROTC program, did nothing to help me.

Fortunately, every time the administrators asked Catherine about her parents' accusations, she always said, "Luke's not bothering me at all. He's my best friend. My parents just don't like him. They don't agree with who he is." Eventually the school dropped the expulsion case. But they continued to keep Catherine and me apart. And anytime a teacher reported that he or she saw us together, Catherine would get hell at home.

The thing that kills me is that her parents' main argument for why I was evil was that the Bible states you're not supposed to alter your body. Meanwhile, I've heard rumors that her mom has had at least one face lift, both her mom and dad have tons of tattoos, and all their children have braces and glasses. It was the definition of hypocrisy.

Catherine and I tried to duck the adults and continue to hang out, but it got to be too hard. Neither of us wanted her to get into trouble at home, so we began to drift apart. It got to the point where we'd see each other in the hallway only occasionally. We'd wave and maybe say hi. But that was it. I missed her desperately, and I knew she missed me, too. But what could we do?

Without Catherine, Maria, and Lisa, I grew closer to my gay friends at OYP. All week I would look forward to Saturday night dances, when I could see Andrea, Brendan, Jeanie, Robbie, and everyone else. One Saturday night I was goofing around, dancing with Andrea, when one of the full-time volunteers came up and asked us if we wanted to be on television to help educate people about LGBT rights. The

Obama administration had just launched a campaign to prevent anti-gay bullying at schools, and the local CNN station
was looking for teens to interview.

"Absolutely," I said.

"Definitely," said Andrea.

I was wearing tight blue jeans and a sheer white blouse
with a white tank top that night, and was feeling pretty cute.
The thought of being on TV as Katie gave me an electrifying
thrill.

"Would your moms be open to talking too? We'd need
them to come meet us right now," the volunteer said.

Andrea and I called our moms.

"I'm on my way," said Mom. "Just give me ten minutes
to do my makeup!"

My mom arrived at OYP, and we were pulled into a van,
along with Andrea and her mom. As we rode over to the
CNN station building, I had fantasies of a fancy television
newsroom set, of being surrounded by cameras and lights.
However, this was not the case. After parking, entering
through some back door, and walking down various hallways and down numerous flights of stairs, we ended up in a
small, creepy storeroom-looking area with a single camera, a
crappy TV, and two guys chowing down on take-out food.

They set up a little cardboard background and sat my
mom, Andrea, her mom, and me down and asked us questions about coming out at an early age. The man interviewing us wasn't really listening and just wanted to get in his
sound bites, but I was able to say things that were important
to me, that I thought could help others.

"People think we choose to be this way. But no one

wakes up and chooses to be hated by everyone."

It was my first taste of advocating, and I was hooked.

Over the previous few months, Ken and Tim and everyone else at OYP had become much more knowledgeable about transgenders, but at this point I still hadn't met any other trans people! I told my mom how I felt, and she found out about this place called the Dennis R. Neill Equality Center—OKEQ—in Tulsa. They had a weekly meeting for transgender people, adults only, but it was something. My mom talked to someone at the center on the phone, and they said that if she came with me, I could join.

It's hard to believe OKEQ was there, only fifteen miles away, all those years I was so confused and suicidal. The first time I walked through its glass doors into the warm, colorful building, with a gift shop featuring rainbow flags, same-sex wedding cake decorations, and coffee cups with the logo OKLAHOMO, I knew my life was going to change. The restroom didn't say "Male" or "Female." It just said "Restroom."

"Hey, can I help you guys?" said a large man with a gray mustache. "I'm Toby Jenkins, 'head homo' here at OKEQ."

"Um, we're looking for the transgender support group?" said my mom.

"Sure thing," said Toby, flashing me a warm smile. "Right this way."

My mom and I entered a room where about twelve people were seated around a foldout conference table. I glanced around at the different faces. For the first time in my life, I was actually in a room with other transgender people. Everyone was much older than me, and I felt a little uncomfortable. I was wearing a black fedora and suddenly panicked that the style choice was a bit much.

"Hello. I'm Dr. Laura Arrowsmith," said a woman with glasses and long gray hair. "I run the transgender programs here at the center."

"I'm Jazzlyn," said my mom, "and this my daughter, Katie. She's transgender. . . . We're still figuring everything out. At least, I am."

"That's fine. Welcome," said Dr. Arrowsmith.

My mom and I took seats, and then everyone went around the circle and introduced themselves.

"I'm Lily," said a woman with poofy black hair who reminded me of Velma from *Scooby-Doo*.

"I'm Maddie," said a large woman who appeared to be balding.

Looking at Maddie made me kind of sad, and I averted my eyes.

"I'm Raj," said an Indian trans man.

"Mary."

"Linda."

Everyone gave their names, and the discussion began. Linda talked about how she was saving up for her surgery. A woman named Samantha said that she was saving up for a nose job as part of her facial feminization. Most of the trans women there were not out in their daily lives. They went to work as men, and expressed as women only in the evenings or on weekends. I began to worry that that would be my fate too. The truth was, though it was exciting to see and hear from other trans people, because of my age I felt pretty alienated from the group. Most of my concerns and questions had to do with transitioning in high school, how other teens would react, what it would be like to start dating. I wasn't sure if this group could help me with that or not.

"Where are you at in your transition, Katie?" Dr. Arrowsmith asked.

"Well, I'm still my old name and gender at school, but I've been dressing and going out as Katie outside of school. I'd really like to start transitioning medically—go on hormones—but I'm not sure where to start." I glanced at my mom.

"I'm trying my best, but I'm at a loss here," my mom said, her eyes starting to tear up. "Is it safe for her to start hormones? Is she ready? I don't know what to do."

"It's okay," said Dr. Arrowsmith. "We're here to help, and you've been amazing just bringing Katie here."

"Wait, I'm confused," said Maddie. "Are you female-to-male or male-to-female?"

Everyone laughed, and a few other people said they couldn't tell whether I was FTM or MTF either. I guess I passed as a girl so well that they weren't sure. Or maybe the fedora had thrown them off.

"I'm MTF," I said.

"Many trans women start taking female hormones—in either pill or shot form—to help change their bodies to look more feminine," Dr. Arrowsmith explained to my mom. "It's a serious medical decision, which is why if Katie does take hormones, she should be under the supervision of a doctor."

"Where would we go for something like that?" asked my mom. "Do they take insurance?"

"Not everyone does, but I can recommend some doctors."

"Dr. Haas is wonderful," said Linda.

"Definitely Dr. Haas," said Mary.

"Thank you all so much," said my mom, looking at everyone. "I can't even tell you . . ."

I looked at my mom and squeezed her hand.

The next day my mom called Dr. Haas's office to try to set up an appointment.

"I'm sorry, but Dr. Haas is no longer accepting new patients," the receptionist told her.

"Okay, but if you'll just let me explain. I've got this child . . . ," my mom said.

I sat there listening to my mom tell my story. My mom gave me a funny look, so I got up and pressed my ear to the phone receiver. The receptionist was crying.

"Hang on one second," she said. My mom was put on hold for a moment, and then the woman came back.

"Bring her in," she said. "Bring. Her. In. We'll figure it out."

The next day my mom drove me to the large, gray medical complex in Tulsa where Dr. Haas has her office. As soon as I sat down with Dr. Haas, a short, sweet woman in her sixties, I launched in.

"I'm transgender," I said. "And I want to start on female hormones."

Dr. Haas smiled and nodded. "Do you see yourself someday having sex reassignment surgery?" she asked.

"Yes," I said. "That's my goal."

"And you understand the steps it takes to get to that point?" Dr. Haas continued.

"Yes. I need to take the Real Life Test and live for two years as the gender I was meant to be, twenty-four hours a day, seven days a week."

I glanced over at my mom, who looked a little bewildered. I don't think she knew exactly how informed on everything I already was. But how could I not be!

"When can I start my hormone treatment?" I asked, turning back to Dr. Haas.

"We can start today if you want," she said.

Dr. Haas looked me over. "I have to say, I find it hard to believe you're 100 percent biologically male. I wouldn't be surprised if you're intersexed. I'd like to run some tests."

I knew that "intersexed" meant someone who, to some degree, had male and female parts. My genitals were not ambiguous—I clearly had a normal penis and testicles—but I did have the small breast growth and other feminine characteristics like curves and barely any facial hair. Maybe intersexed made sense.

Dr. Haas said she was going to order a chromosome test, a hormone level test, and do an ultrasound of my abdomen to see if I had any female internal organs. She also sent me home with my first round of hormones: estrogen by injection, and spironolactone pills. The estrogen was to soften my skin, lengthen my hair, redeposit fat in a female manner, and aid breast growth. My mom had never given shots before, but Dr. Haas showed both of us how. The spironolactone was to inhibit androgen (male hormones) production. I would need to take estrogen for the rest of my life. The spironolactone was necessary only as long as my testes were producing androgens, so if and when I had surgery that removed my testicles, I could then stop taking spironolactone.

Being on hormones for the first time was exhilarating. I was finally on my way to inhabiting the body I'd only dreamed of. My mind swam with images: Would the shape of my face change? How big would my breasts get? Would I be beautiful? More important, would I *feel* beautiful? I wanted one year, two years, three years to already be past so I could see how I would look in the future. Dr. Haas had explained that hormones change each person's body uniquely and at different paces. I hoped they worked on my body quickly.

The day after I had my first shot of estrogen, I experienced my first "female" mood swing. My mom wanted to go shopping, and when I couldn't find my purse, I collapsed onto the ground in a hormonal rage.

"I can't find my purse!" I cried, incredibly frustrated.

It sounds almost like a sexist parody of some girl "PMS-ing," but in the moment, I genuinely felt that tortured. Honestly, the idea that the hormones could have such an effect on my mood excited me—they were working!

I went back to Dr. Haas about a week later to get the results of my various tests. She told me my chromosomes were XY—normal for a male—but that the hormone levels in my blood were highly atypical. Most adult men have testosterone in the range of 300 to 1000 ng/dL (nanograms per deciliter). Mine was at twenty. Meanwhile, my estrogen levels were the same as my mom's. Dr. Haas didn't know why this was, only that my body naturally produced hormone levels closer to a female than a male. She wanted to keep me on the estrogen shots and spironolactone pills, though, to halt any male puberty such as more body hair. The pelvic ultrasound hadn't shown anything irregular inside me, but Dr. Haas said she wanted to take a closer look with a CAT scan.

A few days later I went to the hospital to get the CAT scan done. I had to drink this oral contrast stuff the night before, which was disgusting. The whole experience was incredibly awkward. The technician let me know I'd have my results in a week.

When my mom and I went back to Dr. Haas, she pulled up the report and said, "Katie, you're going to laugh your ass off."

"Okay," I said. "I'm kind of nervous now. . . ." I had no idea what to expect.

"Well, first off, it says you have elongated hips, the hip measurement of an average teenage girl."

"Cool!" I said.

"Also, I'm seeing two dark spots in the location where ovaries would be. It's possible these could be unformed ovaries, but there's no way to know for certain without doing surgery and actually looking inside. If they *are* ovaries, it would mean that you partially developed a second set of sex organs and are intersexed." Dr. Haas paused. "Now here's the funny part. At the bottom the report reads, 'There are two adjacent oval hypodensities measuring two by two-point-five centimeters and two by three-point-three centimeters, respectively, which may represent testicles.'"

"*May* represent testicles?" I said, laughing. "How do you get '*may* represent testicles'?" They were referring to my actual testicles. Apparently the technician hadn't realized I had male sex organs. All he would have had to do was lift up the sheet, and he would have seen that I did in fact have testicles.

Dr. Haas said it was her hunch that I was intersexed, but without further testing we wouldn't know for sure, and if I *was* intersexed, we wouldn't know what form. If you type "intersex" into Google—which of course I'd already done—you'll find that there are about a million and a half different cases. There are people with XXY chromosomes or XO chromosomes, there are people with ambiguous genitals, and people with two sets of internal reproductive organs.

Any further testing, however, would not be covered by insurance. It would be expensive and invasive, and frankly, at that point in time I didn't care what I technically was. I had been a boy my entire life, and all I cared about now was becoming a girl as fast as possible. My mom and I agreed to leave it.

Some people may believe that if I am indeed intersex, I shouldn't identify as trans. I disagree. For me "intersex" falls under the umbrella term "transgender." And my life experience, being raised as male and transitioning to female, has been a transgender experience. Ultimately the human body is a vastly complicated organism, and our tools for understanding it are limited at best.

Intersex or not, I still had a penis, and this was a problem I wanted to remedy as soon as possible. In the months since I'd first come out, I had done a lot of Internet research on transgenderism, and I had learned that, per the World Professional Association for Transgender Health Standards of Care, I would need a letter from a therapist in order to get sex reassignment surgery. Even though I was still wary of therapists, especially after my experience with the one after I first came out, I was willing to do whatever it took to get my surgery. This time I told my mom I needed to find a therapist who specialized in transgenders.

As it turned out, finding a therapist even just familiar with—let alone specializing in—transgender issues proved difficult. My health insurance was Tricare—a military insurance through my dad—and the military is not accepting of most things LGBT. (At the time, Don't Ask, Don't Tell was still in effect, and as of the publication of this book, open transgenders are not allowed to serve in the military.) When my mom called Tricare and tried to explain that she needed a therapist for her transgender child, their response was, "Uh, we don't have anybody like *that*."

"Do you at least have anyone who specializes in teenagers?" my mom asked.

The woman on the phone rattled off a list of male therapists' names.

"What about a woman?" my mom asked. I had been adamant that I wanted to speak with someone female.

They had one name—Dr. Brenda Bowman, a therapist in Tulsa. My mom spoke to Dr. Bowman on the phone, and while Dr. Bowman was hesitant at first because she'd never had a transgender client before, she told my mom to bring me in. If she didn't think she could help me, she'd work with my mom to find someone who could. That would mean paying full cost out of pocket, but my mom said she would figure it out if she needed to.

My mom drove me forty-five minutes to Dr. Bowman's office on Peoria Avenue in Tulsa. I was expecting a building complex housing several therapists, like I'd seen before, but the address we pulled up to was just a small, normal-looking house.

"Are you sure this is the right place?" I asked my mom.

My mom checked the address again and shrugged. "Should be."

We drove around to the driveway, where there were six or seven cars already parked, so unless they were having a party, maybe this *was* a therapy office. We went inside, where a receptionist sat behind a desk in what appeared to be the living room. I looked around at the paintings on the walls and at the homey furniture. It seemed legit, though.

"Brenda will be with you in a few minutes," the receptionist said. "She's heard all about you and is excited to meet you."

My mom and I sat down and waited. I flipped nervously through *Highlights* magazines while my mom looked at *Vogue*. After about thirty minutes I was called back to see Brenda.

Brenda Bowman was in her late forties, tall with brown hair, glasses, and a kind, welcoming face. Her voice was sweet and soft, like honey. I immediately found her calming. She was the furthest thing from stuffy, detached Dr. Ashman. Also unlike Dr. Ashman, whose office was dark and musty, crammed with his books and framed photographs, Dr. Bowman's office was light and airy. The blinds were open so the sun could shine through, and the space was almost bare. There was just the couch, a filing cabinet, a coffee table with a box of tissues and little magnetic beads, and the chair Brenda sat down in. I liked the way her office made me feel. I sat down on the couch and immediately started playing with the magnetic beads. Whenever I talk, especially about my feelings, I like to do something with my hands.

My mom had already sent Brenda all my medical info from Dr. Haas, along with my psychiatric history files. Brenda looked through the files for about five minutes, then said, "Tell me how you feel. How do you feel in your skin?"

No other therapist had ever asked me that before.

"I feel terrible in my skin," I said, answering Brenda's question, playing with the beads. "That's why I'm here. I'm transgender, and I need to go to therapy in order to get my surgery. I need a therapist to say that I'm not mentally crazy but that this is actually a thing. Having this surgery will help me feel better. I'm not just off my rocker doing crazy things." I looked up tentatively.

"No, no, I understand," said Brenda. "I've never encountered a trans person before, but I understand the procedure you have to go through to get surgery, and I've heard a little bit about you and am excited to get to know you more."

"Okay," I said, smiling a little. "Cool."

We didn't delve too much into the trans stuff that first session. Mainly Brenda just got to know me. She asked what my college plans were, how my relationship with my mom was, what I liked to do for fun. They were the same types of questions a new friend might ask you. At that point in time I was still rather antisocial and afraid of people. But just the fact that I was talking to an adult about my life made me feel better. I could talk to Catherine and to my new gay friends at OYP, but socializing with kids is different. I never got the sense when I talked to other teens that they really cared about the details of my life. Brenda asked as if she cared.

Over the next few sessions I fell in love with her. One day she asked me at what age I realized I was a girl. That was the thing—she was always very proper about how she phrased things, careful not to offend me. It wasn't "When did you first *want* to be a girl?" but "When did you first *know* you were a girl?" She had clearly educated herself on what transgenderism is and was very keen on her vocabulary and rhetoric. We discussed how if I did get surgery, it would be painful and expensive. We also just talked about whatever was going on in my life—who I had a crush on, or, as the months passed and I tentatively started dating for the first time, what that was like. After about a year we even got into depth about my sex life. She wanted to make sure I was doing things safely. The most important thing for me was that she made me feel normal, made me feel that despite being trans, I was just like everybody else.

On June 28, 2010—what would have been my mom and dad's seventeenth wedding anniversary—my mom drove me down to the courthouse to legally change my name. I wanted to be sure the judge mediating my name change took me seriously—didn't think I was just confused or joking—so I had taken extra care in selecting my outfit of ironed black pants and blouse and doing my makeup. My mom was just as excited as I was, and even more nervous.

"Make sure you're respectful and don't argue," she said, taking her eyes off the road for a moment to look at me. "Sit up straight. Don't talk back and don't joke!"

"Okay! I know!" I said.

"If they ask why you're doing this, just tell them the truth. Be sincere, don't be afraid. And I will be right there with you."

"Thanks, Mom," I said.

We drove away from the flat farms of the Bixby area and into the dense buildings of downtown Tulsa. Every mile closer we got, I could feel my heart beating faster. This was it. *From now, and forever forward, people will have to refer to me as Katie. I am Katie.*

"They'll have a metal detector, so make sure you don't have anything metal on you," my mom said. "They should give you a bunch of papers after the judge approves the name change, and then we'll go to the Social Security office . . ."

My mom rambled on as I stared out the window, listening to the music on the radio and daydreaming about everyone I knew calling me Katie.

"Huh? I'm sorry, Mom. What were you saying?" I said in a joking tone.

"Katie! This is important."

"I know, I know."

"You ready?" she asked as we pulled into the courthouse parking garage.

"Yes," I said.

We walked through security and took the elevator up to our appointed floor. We had to wait about forty-five minutes until our judge was available. My mom chattered anxiously.

"Do you think the judge will be wearing a black robe and carrying a gavel? Maybe the bailiff will come out and direct us to her. . . . I'm really not sure how this all works."

I, however, felt surprisingly calm and collected.

"It will be fine, Mom," I said.

When our judge came out, I relaxed even further. She was wearing normal clothes and had beautiful red hair and a big grin with very deep smile lines. I liked her instantly. She brought us back to her office, a cylindrical room with an enormous curved bookcase, and sat us down.

"I'm Judge Fuller," she said.

"I'm Katie," I said, shaking her hand.

"Jazzlyn," said my mom.

"And you're here for a name change, correct?" asked the judge.

"Yes," said my mom. She placed her hands in her lap, crossed her legs, and shook her hair behind her neck.

"All right," said the judge. "Now, where is Luke?"

"Luke?" I asked.

"Yes, Luke, the one who's getting the name change. Where is he?" asked the judge.

"Well, um, this is Luke," said my mom with a short chuckle. "She's getting a name change; she's transgender."

"Oh my goodness, I'm sorry!" said the judge. She looked at me. "I thought you were Luke's mother."

Mother? I thought.

"Well, you bet your bottom dollar I am going to sign this," said the judge. "I've got to say, you are a very beautiful lady." The judge quickly scratched some writing on our paperwork and then looked up with a smile. She leaned forward on her elbows and seemed to marvel at me for a second, then looked over at my mom, chuckled, and shook her head in a somewhat disbelieving way. She handed Mom the paperwork. "Here you go. Just take this down to floor one, and they will handle it from there."

We all stood up, and the judge shook Mom's hand and then mine. "It was an honor meeting you, and good luck!" she said.

My mom and I went back into the elevator. She turned to me with a frank smile.

"*Mother?* She thought *you* were the mother? What the hell does that make *me*?"

We laughed all the way down to the first floor.

My mom and I had done it. Almost everything on my list had been ticked off. My name was Katie and I was referred to as "she," I looked and dressed like Katie, I had a support group and had met other trans people, I was on female hormones, and I had applied for a job at a local diner to start saving up for my surgery.

Ever since I'd begun to transition and finally get my life on the right track, I had woken up each morning with new feelings of hope and joy. Despite this happiness, though, I still carried a lot of resentment, particularly toward religion. I missed Catherine, Maria, and Lisa greatly, and I knew their parents had all used God as the reason I could no longer be friends with them, because God sends all LGBT people to hell. And so I hated religion and everything it supposedly stood for. These feelings of hatred churned inside me, until one day I had an experience I can only describe as spiritual.

A few days after getting my name changed, my mom and I were driving down a road in Tulsa. I was in the backseat, staring out the window. I was feeling a bit low, thinking about all the people—my dad, kids at school—who had rejected me for being trans, when I looked up at the sky and saw a cloud, gentle and shaded, in the exact shape of an eye staring directly at me. It was beautiful. I rolled down my window, feeling the warm Oklahoma summer air as I looked back into the eye and it continued to look down at me. Before I knew it, I was crying. I felt flushed with emotion and tingly all over my body, almost dizzy. I closed my eyes and felt this overwhelming sense that I was being hugged and that everything was going to be okay. Who knows, maybe I was just struck with some stray cosmological radiation or some nonsense like that. . . . I'll never know, but as it was happening, I was certain that it was special, that it was caused by something beyond my understanding and possibly beyond the mundane. It was the most incredible thing I'd ever seen, and it changed me. From that moment on I really started to think about things. I stopped hating God and I stopped being bitter toward others and their beliefs. Overall, I just stopped being angry.

As soon as I began to identify as Katie, I started hooking up with boys. "Men" is a more accurate way to put it. Apart from Arin, I've only ever been with older guys. And there have been a lot of them. Unlike most girls, I didn't have a whole lifetime to explore my female identity and figure out my sexuality. I just kind of got pushed into it and had to discover who I liked, what I liked, and what my boundaries were in a very short period of time. Because of that, I went a little overboard. It was pretty much, *You think I'm pretty and want to kiss me? Unless you have mono, okay!* Although I don't want to brag, I have to say, all the guys I've been with have been extremely good-looking.

My first kiss was when I was fifteen, with this twenty-two-year-old bisexual guy named Tony. I had just begun to transition and was feeling really dysphoric.

"No one's ever gonna like me. No one's ever gonna want to kiss me. I'm ugly," I said to Tony in the parking lot of OYP one day.

"Katie," he said, "I think you're beautiful." And he leaned in and kissed me.

The first guy I actually dated was Jeff. I was sixteen. He was twenty-three, short but superhot. Because he was so much older, everyone kind of raised an eyebrow. My mom was okay with it, though, which I think in large part was because she knew I couldn't get pregnant. I look back on it now, and yeah, the age difference was significant, but Jeff never tried to get me to do anything I didn't want to. It pretty much stayed at kissing, and then, after a few weeks, he ditched me for another girl—one his own age.

Then there was this guy Tommy (more making out), and then Saul, who has the distinct honor of having the first penis I ever touched. It was really awkward because he was sleeping over at my house along with my friend Patrick. We were lying on blankets on the floor—Patrick was to my left and Saul was to my right, and I was touching Saul under the covers.

"Now me to you," Saul whispered.

"Nope," I said, and turned around.

Though I was feeling more and more comfortable in my body as a result of the hormone treatment—my breasts and butt were filling out, and my skin was softer—I didn't want anyone touching me where I felt dysphoric. Even Saul just asking made me want to get up, go lock myself in my closet, and cry. No one ever pressured me, but a lot of guys did ask. "I don't care that you're trans. I think you're strong and attractive the way you are," they would say. But it didn't matter. I just didn't want to go there at that point in time. It wasn't until my first real boyfriend—Hawthorne—that I opened up.

I met Hawthorne during the summer of 2010 through my friend Kyle, whom everyone calls Ferris. I actually had a crush on Ferris first. Ferris and I met at Camp Anytown, a summer camp designed to teach teenagers about equality and respect for all people, whether they're gay, straight, Muslim, Jewish, black, white, brown, etc. The camp was a mix of gay, straight, and everywhere-in-between kids. I learned about the camp through OYP, and a bunch of my gay friends were going as "gay delegates" to speak to other campers about gay issues. It sounded fun, and I decided to go too.

I was going through a punk phase at the time, and as soon as we got to camp, I noticed scruffy-cute Ferris, a straight cisgender (non-trans) guy who dressed in tank tops and black Tripps pants. We hit it off, and within a week we were seen as "the camp couple," always flirting and hanging out with each other (though at this point, no making out).

The thing is, I was actually at the camp undercover. Before I'd arrived, the camp officials had asked me not to tell anyone I was trans. My friends at OYP were supposed to keep my "secret" as well. Because I passed so well, they wanted me to blend in for the first week, and then on Gay Day, when all the gay delegates spoke, I was supposed to "reveal" that I was trans and *blow their minds*. The camp officials wanted me to help people understand that transgender people aren't weird or foreign but are actually just like everyone else. I did want to help others learn to accept trans people, so I agreed.

But I couldn't do it. That week, when we canoed and built campfires and went on hikes, was one of the happiest times of my life. Camp Anytown was the first place where I made friends, flirted with guys, lived my life, and had fun as just Katie the girl, not Katie the trans girl. I wanted to educate people, but more than that I wanted to hold on to my new non-trans experience. I told the director I didn't have the heart to come out to everyone. He understood, but I could tell he was disappointed. I didn't care. I knew I had made the right decision.

I did, however, decide to tell Ferris. I really liked him and felt that if we were going to have anything serious, I should be up front about being trans. One morning we both got up early to go on a hike together. We'd been walking in silence for a while, just listening to the birds and sounds of nature, when we came to a clearing.

Okay, this is the perfect place to do it, I thought.

"Should we sit for a bit?" I asked, sitting down on a rock in the clearing.

"Sure," said Ferris, and he sat down next to me.

"So, look," I said. "I just wanted to tell you that I think you're really awesome. I know it's been less than a week, but I've really liked getting to know you."

"You too," he said. "I really like you."

"And, you know, I'm not, like, asking you to date me when camp ends, but I just wanted you to know that I think you're really cool."

And then I leaned in and gave him a quick kiss on the mouth. Truth be told, I was scared that if I told him I was trans first, he wouldn't kiss me, so the order was deliberate.

We broke apart, and he was grinning at me.

"Also . . . ," I said. "There's something you should know about me."

"What?" he said, still with that goofy grin.

"I'm transgender."

"You're what?"

"I'm trans. I was born male and transitioned into being female."

"Whoa, uh, that's a little weird," he said. His grin was still there but had become twisted, almost like he was in pain now.

"I just thought you should know," I said. I could feel myself blushing. *Should I not have told him?* I thought. *No, you needed to tell him.*

"No, I mean, that's cool," he said. But I could tell he was creeped out.

"We should head back," I said.

"Yeah," he said.

We walked back to the camp area, awkwardly making small talk, both of us trying to pretend like the kiss and my coming out had not happened.

The next day was Gay Day, and my friends from OYP, including Andrea, spoke. Afterward Andrea, some other friends, and I were hanging out by the cabins when another friend I had made at camp named Cassie came up.

"Did you hear what that one guy said about accepting trans people?" she said. "I am *not* okay with that. Those people are just weird. You agree, right, Katie? Something's wrong with them."

It was incredibly awkward. Andrea was standing next to me but knew not to out me.

"Trans people aren't weird," Andrea said. "I have trans friends."

"Whatever," said Cassie. "I think they're nasty. They all have mental disorders."

I wanted to correct Cassie, to tell her she was wrong. But I was so caught up in being "just Katie" that I held my tongue.

Two days later my brief time as "just Katie" came to an end. One of the counselors told everyone in her cabin that I was trans, and those people in turn told everyone in the entire camp. And they weren't just saying that I was trans—they were also saying I was an ugly boy trying to be a girl.

Everyone immediately started treating me differently. Kids pointed, stared, laughed, or came up to me and asked inappropriate questions such as, "What do you even have down there? A penis or a vagina?" Ferris told me he didn't mind that I was trans, but it was obvious he did. My gay friends from OYP stood by me, but other than them, I basically felt shunned by the entire camp. I had already been segregated in my own cabin because the gender marker on my ID still read "male," and the camp had said that I either had to bunk in a boys' cabin or in my own. I'd chosen the latter. I spent the remaining few days of camp crying alone in my cabin. I don't know if the camp director knew what had happened, but if he did, he did nothing. For a camp supposedly centered on respect and acceptance, I would have been better off at Camp Prejudice.

When I returned from camp, I told my mom what had happened, and together we caused quite an uproar. The counselor who'd outed me was fired, and the camp director called to personally apologize. Meanwhile, Ferris and I tried to remain friends, but in addition to his discomfort over my being trans, it also turned out that the entire time we'd been at camp, he'd had a girlfriend back home. I guess our camp flirtation had been just a distraction for him. I felt pretty used. We did hang out a few times, though, and one of those times, he introduced me to Hawthorne.

Ferris, my friends Jeanie and Brent (from OYP), Brent's girlfriend, and I had decided to hang out at the Woodland Hills Mall. When we all met up, Ferris was with Hawthorne. Hawthorne was wearing a black tank top, black Tripps, and black Converse. He was skinny, tall enough to be a basketball player, with a thick jaw and short hair. He was definitely cute, if maybe a little rough around the edges—even for me in my punk phase. I wasn't that impressed. I could tell he was sweet deep down, though. His blue eyes had a sadness and kindness in them.

We didn't talk very much that day, but the second time I saw Hawthorne, things were different. It was about a week later, and I'd managed to get over Ferris. My fragile sixteen-year-old self-confidence was more or less back to normal. This time it was just Ferris, Hawthorne, and me, and right from the start we were all laughing and joking. Hawthorne bought me a bag of sour rainbow stripe candy, and we ran around the mall playing games. Ferris gave Hawthorne my phone number, and then the two of them dashed off to hide while Hawthorne texted me clues about where to find them. I bought us all lunch at the food court, and I could tell Ferris was jealous of the way Hawthorne and I were flirting. This pleased me immensely. Eventually Ferris got a call from his girlfriend and had to leave to bike to her house to have sex or something.

Hawthorne and I were left alone. It was awkward at first, but I reacted quickly and suggested we see a movie.

The movie was *The Other Guys,* starring Mark Wahlberg and Will Ferrell, about two cops who get into a mess of trouble. Or something. I barely paid attention. It was such a hot day and so nice and cool in the dark theater, all I wanted to do was take a nap. I asked Hawthorne if it was all right if I laid my head on his shoulder. I *swear* I was really just tired. Eventually my head migrated from his shoulder to his knees. He laid his left leg over his right and angled his hips toward me so I would be more comfortable. I'd been in his lap about five minutes when he leaned down and whispered into my ear.

"You're very special. Do you know that?"

I'd had people tell me I was beautiful or awesome, but never, and never again to this day, had someone told me I was special the way Hawthorne did in that moment. I turned away from the screen and looked up at his face. He wasn't smiling; he wasn't blushing; his face seemed to have no emotion at all. But his eyes stared down at me with this mixture of pity and amazement, like he was looking at a hurt, mythical creature he'd never seen before. His pale face flickered in the light from the movie.

"What do you mean?" I asked.

He didn't say anything, just leaned down and kissed me very slowly. I'd done a lot of kissing, but this was my first *real* kiss. There was a raw emotion behind it that meant something. As I began to kiss him back, I told myself I had to be careful. I had to be sure and guard myself so he wouldn't— *couldn't*—hurt me. I pulled away.

"I can't kiss you," I said.

"Why?"

"Because if you knew the truth about me, you would be disgusted and leave."

Hawthorne finally smiled. "Ferris already told me. He told me everything about you, and I don't care. You're beautiful, funny, witty, and special. That's what I see."

Honestly, I was shocked. We watched the rest of the movie as thoughts zipped through my head. *Is he playing me? Is he lying? Is he plotting to kill me?*

After the movie he took me to the side of the theater.

"Don't worry," he said. "You're something to cherish. I'll call you tonight. I want to see you again."

I watched him walk away as I waited for my mom to pick me up.

Hawthorne and I had been dating a few months when I decided it was time for me to have sex. I say I decided it was "time," but I wouldn't say I was actually really ready. I just thought that because I was sixteen, it was the thing to do. I also saw it as a way to get more attention from Hawthorne. By this point I was crazy about him. He had told me he loved me; he said those words all the time. But somehow, nothing he did or said was ever enough.

He was having troubles at home and had spent the previous few weeks crashing at Ferris's grandma's house. One night we were hanging out in Hawthorne's room there, and I just offered it to him.

"Do you want to have sex?" I asked. I was desperate to feel like he wanted me.

"Yeah!" he said, surprised and excited.

There's all this pressure built up around your "first time"

but mine was a bit sad, to be honest. I made him turn out all the lights and shut the blinds. I was so dysphoric, I didn't want either of us to have to see my body.

I asked if he had a condom, and he told me he was clean, that there was nothing to worry about. I believed him because it was what I wanted to believe.

The whole thing lasted for about an hour. Neither of us made any sound. It was painful, and it felt like what I was doing was wrong. From beginning to end I hated it. But I was willing. I still felt like I was making the right decision, if that makes any sense.

When it was over, I awkwardly scuttled off to take a bath. Afterward I went outside and moped around the front of the house for a while. I felt so confused. All I ever thought about was Hawthorne—he was unquestionably the most important thing in my life—so why hadn't finally having sex with him made me happy?

Eventually I grew to trust him more and was able to enjoy myself during sex. However, because of my dysphoria, I was never able to be truly comfortable the way I wished I could be. It was always more for him. I felt good because I knew he felt good.

12

August 17, 2010. I was doing it. I was returning to Bixby High School for the first day of my junior year, as Katie Rain Hill. I knew that in terms of official enrollment I was still Luke—neither my mom nor I had contacted the school to let them know I was now Katie—but why should that matter? I was ready to introduce and explain myself in person.

I woke up in the morning and got dressed in a pair of blue jeans, a purple shirt, and black flats. I spent about an hour doing my makeup, and my mom let me use her flatiron to straighten my hair. When I looked into the mirror, I felt good. I knew I would be met with some discrimination and hate, but I felt ready to conquer it. *You will not be weak. You deserve to be understood and accepted,* I told myself.

I got into the car with my mom, and we drove the familiar route to Bixby High. She pulled up the school driveway toward the rotunda with the giant blue-and-white *B* sculpture surrounded by three tall, waving flags—for Oklahoma, the United States of America, and the Bixby Spartans. I could feel the terror building inside me. *Oh God, can I really do this? Yes. You belong here, just like everybody else.*

"Have a great day," my mom said, and she leaned in and hugged me.

As soon as I walked through the main doors, I realized I'd had no idea what I was in for. I felt like Lady Gaga dressed in her famous meat-dress surrounded by hungry lions, piranhas, and bears. *Everyone* was staring at me. I took another few steps, and then a football player came up and spat in my face. *"Freak,"* he said, and then walked back to his group of laughing friends. I tried to move past it, ignore it, but everywhere I walked, someone was in front of me, telling me to "Go the fuck home," or pushing me against the wall.

"You make a really ugly girl," one girl sneered, bumping into me as I entered my first class.

It was philosophy, and I went up to the teacher, Mrs. Whiteman. My voice shaking a little, I said, "Excuse me. Can you please not call attention to me today? I want to stay inconspicuous."

"No. Everyone needs to participate. It's not fair to the other students."

"Okay, but it's just, my name is Katie," I said.

Mrs. Whiteman gave me a weird look and nodded. I went and sat down.

"All right, class. I want everyone to stand up and say your name and favorite ice cream flavor."

"Skylar, lemon sorbet."

"Brad, chocolate."

"Melissa, rum raisin."

Oh no, I was next.

"Katie Rain Hill," I said, standing up, attempting to steady my wavering voice. "Mint chocolate chip."

"I have you down as Lukas," Mrs. Whiteman said.

Everyone giggled.

"He's so weird. He's dressed like a girl," I heard a girl in the front whisper to another.

"No, I'm Katie," I said to Mrs. Whiteman.

"I think you should sit down, Lukas," Mrs. Whiteman said.

I could feel myself starting to cry. *No, you* cannot *cry in front of everyone.*

"Can I be excused?" I asked. "I—I need to call my mom."

Mrs. Whiteman sighed. "Yes, you may go to the office."

I turned and walked out the door. The office was down the hall, but I decided that getting some fresh air would be better, so I went outside into the courtyard and took out my cell phone. I hit the speed dial for my mom's cell.

No answer.

I tried her number at work. *Please pick up. Please pick up.*

"Hello?" It was one of the office managers at Food Pyramid.

"May I speak to Jazzlyn, please?"

"One moment."

I waited for a minute or two, watching the double doors to the school, hoping no one else would come out.

"This is Jazzlyn."

"Mom," I said, "I can't do this. I thought I could, but they're tormenting me. . . ." I tried not to cry but couldn't help it. Tears began to build in my eyes.

"Baby, I know. . . . I know it's hard. But you can do it. Just try to get through half of the day. If you can't make it, then I'll come get you, okay?"

My mom's voiced soothed me. I still wasn't sure I could make it, but I felt a little better.

"Okay, I'll try," I said, and we hung up.

I took a deep breath and counted to ten. *One, two, three, four, five, six . . . at ten you go in and face them . . . seven, eight, nine, ten.*

I headed back in through the double doors. By the time I was back in the hall, the class bell was ringing. I had five minutes to get to my next class, and I needed my bag, which I'd left in philosophy. I ran back to the classroom. Everyone had left, and Mrs. Whiteman was stacking papers. My bag was nowhere to be seen.

"Excuse me. Where did my bag go?" I asked, panicking. I glared at Mrs. Whiteman.

"I don't know," Mrs. Whiteman said coolly. "I think another one of the students took it." She returned to stacking papers.

I felt rage building inside me, but what could I do? I didn't have time to look for it. At least it contained only my books and pencils. I still had my wallet and phone. I turned around and hustled to get to my next class, which was in the English wing on the other side of the school. I was hurrying down the steps when I suddenly felt a jolt forward. Someone had pushed me. I stumbled and managed to break my fall against the stairwell wall. I looked behind me and saw two boys, a black kid in a blue T-shirt and a white boy with stringy brown hair, both laughing. They walked past me, and the kid in the blue shirt flashed me a wicked grin. I thought about reporting them to the office, but that had never worked before. And I didn't even recognize either of them. I took another deep breath, ignoring my impulse to just call my mom again.

"You can do this," I said aloud to myself, alone in the stairwell.

I felt a pang of longing for Catherine, Maria, and Lisa— my crew who had always protected me.

I also knew that sitting in his office, on school grounds, the whole time this was happening to me, was my dad. But he was not someone I could go to either.

I made it to English on time, and that class was a bit better, but not much. The whole time I sat there, I could hear laughing and teasing, and I felt small pieces of paper hitting me.

During lunch I decided to try to look for my backpack. I checked the lost and found. No luck. Then the front office. No luck. Then the gym. No luck. I decided to go back to the science building, where my philosophy class had been, to see if someone had returned it to the office there. As I was walking down the hall, I noticed a teacher coming down the opposite side with something hanging from his shoulder.

"My backpack!" I said, jogging up to him.

"Is this yours?" he asked.

"Yes! I've been looking everywhere for it. Someone stole it from my first-hour."

The teacher handed me my bag. "It was in the boys' restroom," he said with a curious tone.

I could feel tears stinging my eyes again. *Of course, the*

boys' bathroom. What a cruel and clever middle finger someone had just given me.

"Thank you," I said, and draped the bag over my shoulder just as the next bell rang. I was starving from not having
eaten lunch, but now I needed to get to Spanish.

I made it through to the end of the day, but just barely.
The teasing and taunting during my classes continued, and
the hallways between class were worse. Girls would come
up to me and say, "How's the penis?" before giggling and
running off down the hall.

"So when did you get your balls cut off?" yelled a boy,
smacking his gum.

At one point a group of girls made crosses with their
fingers as I passed. Within just a few hours it felt like the
entire school was talking about me. I received a text from
Catherine: *Kirsten Young is calling you a chick with a dick.*

I knew Catherine meant well by informing me about
what people were saying, but frankly, it did not make me
feel better. Especially since she wasn't there to stick up
for me.

At the end of the day, my mom picked me up and we
drove away from the school, through the poor, ramshackle
area of town that surrounds Bixby High's sprawling buildings.

"How did it go, baby?" she asked.

"I'm never going back," I said.

Days later I enrolled in Oklahoma Virtual High School. If
I had to describe virtual school in one word, it would be
"bleak." Pretty much the only good thing was that I was able
to sleep in a little, till nine a.m., sometimes ten. After that it

was just the long, lonely stretch of day in which I attended school by myself on my computer. Some days I never even bothered to change out of my pajamas.

I'd turn the computer on and log into the system, and there would be six tabs: math, history, English, psychology, sociology, and Spanish. I'd click on one tab, and a bunch of modules for that subject would pop up. I'd click on "Section One," and there would be a recorded lecture or PBS documentary or article to read with some notes on the bottom. The next link would contain examples of questions and answers. The next link: more examples. The next link: a multiple-choice quiz. I'd have thirty timed minutes to take the quiz. "Congratulations! You got 100 out of 100." Move on to section two. It felt like the sections never ended.

I didn't know any other teens doing virtual school, so I had no one to talk to about it. If I needed help, I was supposed to contact a tutor through instant message. I'd click on a link that listed various "teachers" in different subjects. I'd select one, and then be told, "You're on hold. Your tutor, Mr. Caan, will be available in twenty-two minutes." Often I'd be taking a timed quiz and would have only twenty minutes left, so if I didn't understand a question, waiting for a tutor was useless. Not to mention, a lot of the time a tutor would have no idea what I was talking about anyway, and I'd have to try out three or four tutors until I landed on one who did. That could take more than an hour. Math was the easiest; most math tutors knew what an isosceles triangle was and could easily explain it. But if I tried to talk about abstract concepts in psych or sociology, forget it. I remember once while working on a sociology section, I read an article about "doing gender," which of course fascinated me. But when I tried to talk to a tutor about it, the tutor just typed back: "What is 'doing gender'? I've never heard of that."

"It's on my screen," I typed back.

"I can't look at your screen."

It was hard to stay self-disciplined. I'd study for four hours, then go on Facebook, then study twelve minutes, then think, *I'm hungry,* and go look for food in the cabinet. Then I'd use the restroom. Then it would be three p.m. and Jake would get home from school, and I'd help him with his homework. Mom would come home at five p.m., and we'd have dinner. At seven p.m. I'd still have thirty sections left to do and would stay up until late finishing. Then I'd get up in the morning and do it all again.

I was dating Hawthorne, and that was exciting and going well, but he went to Union High in Broken Arrow, which was forty-five minutes away, so our relationship mainly consisted of talking on the phone and occasionally hanging out on the weekends. I wanted to impress Hawthorne, not have him pity me, so I rarely went into how down I was feeling and instead kept our conversations light. I saw my friends from OYP and OKEQ on the weekends too, but they also all went to faraway schools. For that entire time my primary source of social interaction was Facebook. I'd always spent time by myself, but without the everyday hustle and bustle of school, I was cripplingly lonely.

I had thought that coming out would make everything okay. I was finally me and was able to interact with everybody as my true self. But instead of living the new, social life I'd dreamed of, I found myself back in my stark bedroom, the place I'd so desperately worked to escape. *Screw this,* I'd think, back cramped and eyes raw from staring at the computer screen all day. *I'd rather get bullied than have to sit here and deal with this nonsense.*

Just as I was reaching my breaking point of loneliness, Hawthorne's life fell apart as well. When I'd met Hawthorne, I'd known his home life was troubled, but it wasn't until a couple of months in that I realized just how bad it was. He'd been held back his junior year for skipping class, so he was eighteen when he started as a senior, which is exactly when his mom kicked him out.

"You're not my problem anymore. You're an adult now," she told him.

He couch surfed for a while or slept on park benches, still trying to make it to school and his job at Oliveto's, an Italian restaurant. One night in November, right around Thanksgiving, he actually broke down and started crying on the phone.

"I just don't know what to do or where to go," he said.

"Maybe you could stay with me," I said. The thought of Hawthorne moving in with me made my heart leap with excitement.

"You think?" he asked.

I went to my mom and begged her to let him move in with us.

"No way," she said.

"Are you talking about that Gothic Slipknot guy?" Jake jeered in the background.

"*Shut up,*" I said to Jake, and then in a sweet voice to my mom I said, "Mom, please! He's got nowhere to go! He has a job and he's just trying to finish school." I'm pretty sure I cried.

My mom's face softened. "He can stay under two conditions," she said. "One, he cannot sleep in your room. We'll set up a pallet for him in the computer room. And two, he's got to transfer to Bixby High, because there is no way I'm driving back and forth from Broken Arrow every day. As soon as he graduates, he's out."

I threw my arms around my mom in the tightest hug.

A few days after Hawthorne moved in, I heard some enraging news. Catherine called me to say that my old history teacher, Mr. Leder, was showing his class the YouTube video of my segment on CNN and having everyone laugh at it. "This is ridiculous!" he said to them. "To think I had him in a class!"

I told my mom, and she confronted the school. Mr. Leder admitted to everything, but the school administration did nothing. They noted that I wasn't a student there anymore, which apparently exonerated Mr. Leder.

That incident was the furious push I needed, and my courage was sparked. I told my mom I wanted to re-enroll at Bixby for the spring semester, and no one was going to stop me. Also, Hawthorne was enrolling at Bixby High that semester too. I would have my boyfriend with me.

This time my mom wanted to be certain the school knew about my transition from Luke to Katie and was prepared to protect me from bullying. A couple of weeks before the second term began, she went to the Bixby High administration to talk to them and make sure they were ready for me to come back. Their response was that I was not welcome back. The principal told my mom that because Bixby had only male and female restrooms, no unisex, it was too complicated for me to be a student there. My mom suspected that the real reason was that they knew I would be bullied and they didn't want their football players getting in trouble because of me. It was easier to just not let me back. Mom's and my response? *Screw that.*

My mom went to Toby Jenkins, director of OKEQ, who used to work as a representative at the district attorney's office and who had a lot of experience lobbying for gay rights in DC. As soon as she told Toby what the administration had said, he pulled out law books and pages and pages of legislation. He made photocopies for my mom, marking the relevant passages with Post-it notes.

"By law they have to educate her," he said, handing my mom the giant stack. "Bring them this."

Three days before school was set to start, my mom went back to the principal and told him what Toby had told her.

"No," the principal said. "We don't have to."

My mom slammed Toby's stack of papers down on the principal's desk. "If you think that, then apparently you've got some reading to do," she said. "And I advise you to start now. This is Friday, and my daughter will be at school Monday, and if you don't educate my child, I will *shut this city down.*"

"Well, I guess you've done your homework," he responded.

"If you want to battle me, we'll battle, but I'll tell you

right now, I will win. I've got a whole team of attorneys just waiting for me to pick up the phone."

Monday morning arrived, and I was in my room, getting dressed in black jeans and my favorite red V-neck, when my mom came in with surprising news. She told me she'd just found out that the school had hired their own lawyer and called an emergency board meeting early that morning, mandatory for all teachers and staff, to discuss me. Apparently one of the teachers present had been my dad. He had called my mom to let her know.

"Did Dad stick up for me?" I asked, already knowing that the answer was probably no. He and I still didn't talk. Many people at school didn't even know I was his child.

"I don't know what your father did in the meeting," my mom said diplomatically, "but he cared enough to call me. He told me that the lawyer explained to everyone that I was right. You are going to school today, and they will do everything they can to accommodate you. You'll use the faculty bathroom, so there's no fuss over that, and you will be assigned two members of Bixby High's anti-bullying Safe Team to monitor those around you. Are you ready?"

"Just let me finish my makeup," I said with grin.

"Is Hawthorne ready?" she asked.

"Hawthorne's probably still sleeping," I said.

My mom sighed loudly. "Hawthorne!" she yelled, and headed over to wake him in the computer den.

My mom dropped Hawthorne and me off outside school, and we headed toward the big double doors together. I had many conflicting thoughts swimming through my brain. On the one hand, I was determined not to let the bullies win this time, and Hawthorne's presence gave me confidence. On the other hand, he was this dirty punk kid and could be targeted for bullying himself. I really wasn't sure how people would react to us.

"This school is full of assholes and bitches," I warned him as I pushed the heavy doors open.

"Can't be worse than the dickheads at Union," he said.

As we walked down the hall, I could see people staring and pointing at me as usual.

"Freaks," said a boy in a Bixby High hoodie.

But Hawthorne and I just ignored him, and then we kissed good-bye. I headed toward my first class, and Hawthorne headed toward the back building where the Alternative School classes were held. Because he had been kicked out of his house and was living with us, he was enrolled in the Alternative School, for kids with troubled home situations.

Like my first day the previous semester, this day was difficult. In class, teachers used my old name, Luke, even though they had been informed to use "Katie." Kids still yelled things and spat on me in the hallways. Because Hawthorne was in the Alternative School, we didn't even see each other until the end of the day. Knowing he was close did help, though. Also, despite the taunting and bullying that even Bixby's Safe Team couldn't prevent (though their presence did make *some* difference), there was no question in my mind that I was going to tough this out. I was *not* going back to virtual school. *No* one was going to scare me away this time.

When I woke up the next morning, I dreaded going back but forced myself to anyway. And then I went back a third day, and then a fourth, and before I knew it, several weeks had gone by and I didn't dread going to school anymore. I actually looked forward to it.

When I was Luke—a feminine, nerdy boy—kids teased me because I was different and because they didn't understand who or what I was. And at the time, I didn't understand who or what I was either. Now, though, I knew who I was. I was Katie, a transgender girl, and I was eager to let people get to know me. A new kid would come to school, and I'd go up and say, "Hi, I'm Katie. I'm trans." And most of the time people would be cool with it. I learned that when you're up front and confident about yourself, you're often treated with respect. This is not always the case, of course. There will always be bullies. But the difference between my being confused Luke and confident Katie was phenomenal. I let people know it was okay to ask me questions. If there was something they didn't understand about transgenderism and they asked respectfully, I was happy to answer.

I'd made some new good friends—Adele and Stephanie—in my Spanish class, and one day I was at lunch eating with them when Skylar came and sat down with us. At first my body tensed. Skylar was the popular girl who, sophomore year when I was Luke, had dubbed me Lucy. She used to come up to me in the hallways and say things like, "How's the penis today?" or "Are you on your period yet?" So far this semester she'd mainly ignored me. But now here she was, chatting with Adele and Stephanie about Mr. Schumacher, this English teacher they loved.

"He's so cute! Don't you love all the veins in his arms?" Skylar said.

"Ew! The veins are the only gross part," Stephanie answered.

"Veins can be hot," I said. "As long as they don't poke out too much."

"See," said Skylar, "Katie agrees!"

It warmed my heart to hear her call me Katie.

"I heard he was dating Ms. Carrel, though," I said. "So, good luck."

"Ms. Carrel! Noooo," they all exclaimed.

"You know, you're pretty cool," Skylar said, turning to me. "So, like, you're just a girl now?"

"Yep!" I said. "I'm transgender. I was always a girl, but I was born with male parts. I had to figure it out myself and transition."

"So does that mean you've had surgery, or . . . ?"

Usually it bothered me when people asked me about surgery—it's a really personal question and implies that genitals are the most important part of gender, which they're not—but I knew Skylar meant well and that she was just trying to understand me.

"I hope to one day," I said.

"This all just makes so much sense now," she said. "I totally had you pegged wrong. I thought you were this weirdo, but you're really just a girl. I get it now. We should hang out. Can I get your number?"

"Sure," I said.

We took out our phones and exchanged numbers right there.

And then I murdered her.

Just kidding!

13

FAMILY OF FIVE

The first few months of Hawthorne's living with me were bliss. I mean, it's every teenager's fantasy, right? You're obsessed with this guy, he finally becomes your boy-friend, and then, the next thing you know, he's *living* with you.

One night that sticks out in particular is an evening we spent together right around Christmas, when he'd been living with us for about a month. It was an especially cold snowy night, and my mom wanted to take Jake and me to go see Christmas lights, a family tradition. We nor-mally go to the lights in Honor Heights Park, one of the larger parks in the Muskogee area, but that was more than an hour away, and Mom was nervous about driving on the icy roads, so we decided to see the lights at the local church, Rhema.

"Is it okay if I invite Hawthorne?" I asked.

"Of course," said Mom. "We're not going to just leave him here."

I went into the computer den, where Hawthorne's bed was set up. He was playing a video game.

"Feel like seeing some Christmas lights?" I asked. I hadn't realized until I asked, but I was scared he might say no.

"I'd love to," he said, turning off the game.

I went to my room and got changed to go out. I wanted to dress up especially nice. I did my makeup—tastefully, with a little smoky color around the eyes—and then bundled up in black leggings and a long black skirt with an asymmetrical line. I put on a black shirt, knee-high boots, and my mom's black heavy jacket with a tan belt. When I went out into the living room, I was pleased to see that Hawthorne had put on nice button-down shirt as well.

We got into the car and drove to pick up Jake's friend Paul, and then over to Rhema. The five of us spent the night drinking hot chocolate and marveling at the dancing lights. The opening walkway was adorned with a long archway of blinking lights that were synchronized with Christmas music playing nearby. We laughed and giggled as we took pictures next to the oversize American flag and snowman made of Christmas lights. At one point Hawthorne and I separated from the rest and held hands as we gawked at the shimmering icicles on the trees around the church.

"Okay, now let me get a photo of you in front of those outhouses," said Hawthorne.

"You are such a dork," I said. But I laughed and posed in front of the outhouses anyway.

"Beautiful," said Hawthorne, snapping photos with his phone. "Simply beautiful."

I flicked my now freezing hot chocolate at him playfully, and he flicked his back at me. It felt so good to be there with him and my family.

We drove home, and after Hawthorne went to sleep, I stayed up until midnight chatting with my mom, telling her all my feelings about him.

"I really feel in love," I said.

"I know you do, baby," she said.

The honeymoon period couldn't last forever, though. Shortly after moving into my mom's house, Hawthorne was fired from his job at Oliveto's. We thought it was just a minor set-back—bad luck and a mean boss—but he was swiftly fired from his next job as well. And then fired from the next one. He would go on to be fired from about four more.

My mom asked him all the time to help around the house and mow the yard, but he never did. I'm ashamed to say that I usually sided with Hawthorne and didn't ask him to help out as well, because I wanted him to like me.

At first he and I would go out to the movies or to dinner together, but I was always the one paying. Because he kept getting fired, he never had any money, and I couldn't afford to keep paying for both of us. I was working, but that money was supposed to go toward saving for my surgery. Pretty soon we never went out at all and just spent the majority of our time lounging around the computer den playing *Uncharted 2* on my PlayStation 3. Sometimes this girl Abby, whom Hawthorne was also dating—a detail I stupidly chose to ignore—would come over too, and he'd try to get me to convince my mom to let her spend the night. I know, it sounds horrible. But despite everything, he was sweet to me, and I genuinely believed he cared for me. I was just beginning to live my life as Katie and was still painfully insecure. I didn't think anyone else would ever love me. I liked that Hawthorne was dependent on me. It meant he couldn't leave.

I was so obsessed with Hawthorne, I didn't consider how his presence affected my mom and brother. My mom already had so much to take care of with Jake and me, and now Hawthorne was like a third child. And Jake was given an "older brother" whether he liked it or not. Hawthorne was often rude to Jake, taunting him and bossing him around. I never really stood up for Jake, which, as with Hawthorne's relationship to my mom, I'm ashamed of now. Even though Jake and I were not close and still bickered constantly, he actually came through for me during this time in a lot of ways. Of the people close to me, Jake had been one of the best at segueing into calling me Katie and using "she." Once Jake switched my pronouns, he never slipped up. I had finally gotten my driver's license (after failing—twice!), and Jake knew I desperately wanted a car, but Mom couldn't afford it. Every year my dad bought Jake a new motocross bike, but that year Jake convinced Dad to buy me a car instead—a white Saturn Coupe (that Hawthorne ended up crashing twice).

To round out our happy family at the time, my mom's boyfriend, Dennis, was also living with us. Before I give details about him, I should explain a phenomenon on my mom's side of the family known as the "Geurin Curse." ("Geurin" is my mother's maiden name.) We are a cursed family. We think it's because my mom's folks come from some bad people and this is our punishment. We're of German descent, and though I'm

not totally positive, I believe there's documentation somewhere that we're descendants of one of Hitler's right-hand
men. According to the Geurin Curse, no female can have a
healthy romantic relationship. Whoever she is with, either
the person will die or something really messed-up will happen
to them. It has not failed yet. My grandma's husband got
crushed by a crane. My mom's first husband, who drank and
cheated on her all the time, ended up getting into a crazy car
accident. My mom's next husband forced my mom to choose
between her son Josh and him, and my mom chose Josh. And
then there's my dad, and you know how that ended. Then
she started dating Dennis.

When my mom first met Dennis, he was a good-looking
guy—forty-one, fit, and muscular. At the time, I was fifteen
and had just come out. Three months into their whirlwind
romance, my mom informed me that Dennis was moving in.
I was not thrilled.

"You've got me, who's just starting to transition, and
Dennis doesn't even know," I said to her. "You've got Jake,
who's ten, and needs tons of attention. You haven't had a
serious relationship since Dad, and now this guy's just moving in?"

"Katie, if you and Jake really don't want him to move in,
I will not force this on you," she said.

My mom had been through so much and had made so
many sacrifices. I could tell she really wanted this.

"No, Mom, it's all right. If he makes you happy, then I
want him to move in. You've gone through a lot, and you've
given up a lot for Jake and me. Jake and I can do the same
for you."

So we basically moved Dennis's entire house into our small house. And it was great for a while. He and my mom were really happy, and he was like a stepdad to Jake and me. But then, sure enough, about eight months into the relationship, Dennis got brain cancer.

We first noticed something was wrong when he started sleepwalking and saying things that didn't make a damn bit of sense—talking about building airplanes out of toothpicks, and stuff like that. He would just talk out of his head. We finally convinced him to go to the doctor, and the doctors told him he had a brain tumor. They said it was possible he had gotten it from his time serving in Iraq, where he'd been exposed to a lot of UV radiation. I think it could also be related to all the IED attacks he'd been involved in. He'd had surgery on both his legs because of those. By the time he was diagnosed, the cancer was huge. The doctors told us he'd had it for about eight months—pretty much exactly the length of time he'd known my mom. "Oh, Jesus Christ," my mom said. "The Geurin Curse strikes again."

Dennis started chemotherapy. He'd make jokes about how the chemo made his urine glow in the dark. He also had an unusual reaction, which is that instead of the chemo making him nauseous the way it does most people, Dennis did nothing but eat. He ate everything in sight and ended up gaining around three hundred pounds. If you put two photos of him together—when he and my mom first started dating, and after the chemo—you wouldn't believe it.

Shortly after Dennis was diagnosed, someone else came into our home for several months. Cary Aspinwall, a journalist from *Tulsa World*, contacted me about doing a feature on my transition. She'd heard about me because of my CNN interview. It's pretty funny—in those early years of my transition, I still had a lot of anxiety about people judging me. On bad days I wouldn't leave the house because I was scared someone might say, "That's an ugly girl," or "She's got a big nose," or just plain come up and hit me. But as soon as a newsperson said, "We want to put you on TV or in the newspaper," I was immediately like, "Yeah!" The lure of being a celebrity—fortune, fame, and the chance to help others—trumped my fears of discrimination.

My mom was more hesitant. She thought people might read the article, come find our house, burn it down. But we talked about it, and she said, "You know, we should probably do this. We have an opportunity to help people like you or help people understand transgenders. It's the right thing to do."

Unlike most of the reporters involved in the media attention that would come my way in the future, Cary took her time. She, along with a film crew from *Tulsa World*, spent months coming to our house and interviewing my mom, Hawthorne, and me. The film crew was filming a video segment for the newspaper's website. I loved the attention and the way the interviews allowed me to be more introspective about my life and feelings.

The article was published a few days before my seventeenth birthday. Along with the print version, I had my own page with the video segment up on *Tulsa World*'s website. When I watched it, I felt amazing. I was someone whose story was important enough to share with the world. The article and video had been up for only a couple of hours when Toby Jenkins called.

"Oh my God, Katie. OKEQ is getting hundreds of phone calls from people wanting to know more about transgender people and our programs. We're getting dozens of calls from trans people themselves who are just now, because of your article, coming out. You have no idea how big this is."

When I hung up the phone, my hand was shaking from excitement.

14

THE BIGGEST NEWS

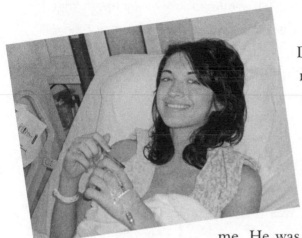

During the summer before my senior year, a few months after the *Tulsa World* article had run, a fashion designer from Tulsa contacted me. He was organizing an event at a Jewish summer camp for teenagers on the topic of judgment, and he wanted me to speak. At this point I'd been out as trans for a year and a half, and passed as a girl easily. I'd refined my taste in clothes and had honed my makeup skills, and the hormones had softened my skin and rounded out my features. Every day I liked how I looked more and more. I was genuinely beginning to see myself as pretty. The fashion designer said that he wanted me to present myself not as transgender but as a regular girl— someone who people might assume had never experienced judgment. Then I would come out to the campers as trans and explain how I *had* experienced judgment. It was a similar idea to what Camp Anytown had wanted me to do, but now, with my confidence bolstered by the success of the *Tulsa World* article, I wanted to participate. The designer introduced me to two girls from the camp to plan the event.

The two other girls, Sophia and Ari, were models, and we decided to make a video in which we were all depicted as models. Sophia would talk about being called names like "slut" and "bitch," and Ari would talk about being judged for having an eating disorder. The video would not reveal why I had been judged, but then I would get up onstage and give a speech on coming out as trans.

What I thought would be a short speech ended up lasting almost two hours. I basically told my whole life story, and there were dozens of questions during the Q&A. Everyone was fascinated. Afterward a lot of the teens came up and wanted to talk to me more. Several adults came up too and told me my message was inspirational and that they were going to speak to their clients and partners in business about me, to make sure my message and story could get to others.

Standing there, surrounded by people waiting to talk to me, to thank me for sharing my story, was when I realized I could make a difference. And maybe not just for trans people. No matter who we are or what we are, what color we are or what's between our legs, we're all just people trying to survive.

I decided that if any more speaking opportunities came my way, I would unequivocally answer *yes*.

The next opportunity that arrived was during the fall of my senior year of high school. Toby called to invite me to speak on a panel about LGBT rights and to give a small speech about my personal story at the University of Oklahoma. Hawthorne had recently run my white Saturn Coupe into a telephone pole, but it was back from the shop, as good as new, and I looked forward to the long drive by myself to Oklahoma City.

"Uh-uh," my mom said. "I am not having you drive two hours on your own."

"What? Why?" I said. "I'll be fine! I'll drive safe!"

"No way. I'm driving you. And besides . . . I want to hear you speak!" she added.

It was a Saturday morning, and my mom and I left super-early, giving ourselves extra time to get to OU, just in case. On the way there we chatted about everything going on in our lives.

"I'll be honest with you, Katie," she said. "That Hawthorne is driving me crazy."

"He's not that bad."

"Actually, he is. Would it kill him to wash a dish or two? The boy is just plain lazy."

"He said he's applying for another job."

"He's been saying that for weeks. And what about Abby? Is he still dating her, too?"

"Abby's over," I said. "I think."

"Mm-hm," my mom said with a smirk.

"How's Dennis?" I asked, wanting to change the subject.

My mom sighed. Dennis had undergone surgery to remove the tumor from his brain, but in the meantime the cancer had spread to his lymphatic system. He had moved out of our house and lived at his mom's when he wasn't at the hospital.

"I don't know what the brain surgery did, but he's got this impulse-control problem now," my mom said. "He spent more than a thousand dollars on iTunes games last month. Anyway, I'm visiting him at his mom's next Friday. I'm honestly not sure how much longer I can do this. But for now I'm sticking by him."

Once we reached the OU campus, I wasn't entirely sure where we were supposed to go, so I called Toby on my cell.

"Hey, Toby. I'm here on the campus. Where should I go?"

"Just head straight to the center building," he said.

"The OU campus is pretty big. . . . Which building is at the center?"

"What road are you on?" he asked. "You should be on Yale."

"I don't know what road I'm on— Wait, did you say 'Yale'? Yale Avenue in *Tulsa*?"

"Yes, right by the Promenade mall."

"Oh my God, Toby. I'm in Oklahoma City! I thought you meant the actual OU campus, not the Tulsa one!"

I glanced over at my mom, who looked like she was suppressing a giant scream. Her eyes were rolled back, and her head was tilted upward, resting on the seat. "Katie . . . ," she began slowly, and then she lost it and started yelling. "I just spent a bunch of money on gas, and now you're telling me we have to drive *all the way* back to *Tulsa*! I can't *believe* you didn't clarify with Toby where we were going!"

I already had a sinking feeling of disappointment, and my mom was making it worse. I hate when she gets mad at me.

Apparently Toby could hear my mom through the phone, because he started talking. "Katie, Katie, listen. It's my fault. I should have clarified. Tell your mom I will repay her for the gas. There are still a couple of hours left of the panel. If you two hurry, you may be able to make it for the last few minutes."

Toby and I hung up. "He says we can make it if we leave now," I told my mom.

"No. I just need to go home and relax," she said, turning the car on. "I'm done for the day."

"Okay, fine," I said, trying to hide how hurt I was. Even though it had been an honest mistake, I felt terrible for wasting her time.

We drove back to Bixby in silence, me listening to my iPod and staring out the window.

When we arrived home, my mom went straight to her bedroom, and I texted Toby to see if the panel was still going on.

Thirty minutes left! Can you make it for the Q&A? he texted back.

Yes! I texted. I ran outside, hopped into my car, and burned rubber to Tulsa.

Fifteen minutes later I was there. Toby was waiting outside the central building to lead me in.

"There's actually just enough time for you to give a quick five-minute summary of your experience before the Q&A," he said.

"Great!" I said as he opened the doors to an amphitheater with a few dozen people in the audience. Onstage stood a group of five teens. I recognized Robbie and Trina from when I'd first started going to OYP, and I waved to them.

Toby went to the podium. "Ladies and gentlemen, I would like to present the lovely Katie Rain Hill," he said.

I walked up to the podium. "Hello! Thank you so much for having me, and I'm sorry I'm late. As Toby said, my name is Katie Rain Hill. I'm seventeen and a senior at Bixby High School." I gave a brief summary of my story, talking about my depression during childhood, coming out at age fifteen, and having to drop out of school my junior year because of bullying.

"When I first came out, my dream was to go stealth as a woman," I said. "I wanted to forget I was ever born male, forget that I was trans, and have people view me just as Katie, an average girl, nothing more. My feelings on that have changed, however. As I've become more confident in myself and overcome many of my doubts and worries, I've realized how important it is to me to be active in the LGBT community. I want to be there for others."

The room filled with gentle applause and smiles. All the panelists sat down for a Q&A, and a number of the questions were directed toward me. People wanted to know about my hope to get gender reassignment surgery, my relationship with Hawthorne, and my plans for the future. After the Q&A a girl a little younger than me came up along with her mother.

"Hi. My name is Kysha," she said, extending her hand. "I read your story in *Tulsa World* and heard you were going to be on this panel, and have been so excited to meet you."

"It's great to meet you, too," I said.

"I go to a private Catholic high school in Tulsa," she said. "It's pretty much hell."

"I can imagine. . . . Hey, if you ever want advice or help or anything, let me give you my number."

"Awesome! Thanks."

We took out our phones and exchanged numbers.

"So you're graduating this year," Kysha said. "You must be excited."

"Oh my God, I can't wait," I said.

I was going to be the first openly transgender student to graduate from high school in Oklahoma. As it would turn out, Kysha would be the second.

More requests for speaking engagements at high schools, youth centers, and colleges came in, and I soon started to feel a bit like a local celebrity. When I walked down the street, people would often stop me to tell me they'd read my *Tulsa World* article and how it had opened their eyes or that they knew someone going through something similar. Sure, some people still hated me, thought I was the devil's spawn dragging everyone to hell and nonsense like that, but in general I walked around town with my head held high. I went to school, and I felt respected.

Sadly, some of the people who had not come around were the parents of my former best friend, Catherine. I even heard that they were handing out a pamphlet with my photo on it, telling people at their church to stay away from me. Suffice it to say, Catherine and I had barely seen each other since sophomore year. However, while Catherine was banned from my classes, Lisa and Maria weren't. So I occasionally ended up in the same class as one of them, though we were still estranged.

One day in marketing class Maria and I were put into a group together to work on a project. There was a moment

when the other members got up and it was just the two of us sitting at the table.

"You know, I'm really, really sorry," she said. It was funny. I was sitting there, a completely different person, but she was the same old Maria—short hair, ruddy cheeks, baggy long-sleeve shirt.

"For what?" I asked.

"I didn't get it. It kind of scared me. And I see now that you're a much happier person. And you're gorgeous. And you're comfortable. I'm sorry I didn't understand, and I just want you to know I'm really proud of you, and I really want to be your friend again."

I almost started crying, right there in class. "I can't be friends with a freak," she had said. I'd really thought I'd lost her forever. And honestly, though I had been angry at first, I understood why my transition had scared and confused her. You can't expect everyone to just immediately empathize with you. But now, having Maria's support again made me feel like I could do anything.

"Thank you," I said. "I've missed you."

Despite being so much happier and more comfortable with myself, there was still one thing that consumed me: getting that penis off my body *now*. As I've said, surgery is not imperative for all trans people; some are content or prefer to live with the genitals they were born with. But this wasn't the case for me.

Surgery was not unfamiliar in my family. My mom had had a boob job. My older half brother, Derik, had had liposuction. Jake had had his ears pinned back. All of their

surgeries combined, however, weren't even half the cost of GRS. I obsessively researched all the different surgeons who performed vaginoplasty, and I kept coming back to the first name I ever heard: Dr. Marci Bowers in San Mateo, California. Dr. Bowers was trans herself, which I liked, and her reviews were overwhelmingly positive. The cost was around thirty thousand dollars. My mom told me, "You keep working part-time, and I will save up what I can, but the reality is that you are going to have to graduate college and get a well-paying job before we'll be able to afford this."

Every day after school and on weekends, I worked first in a diner and then at a fast-food joint to save money. The diner had been dull and tiresome, but I loved my job at the fast-food restaurant. Everyone knew I was trans and was supersupportive. It was a bunch of old men, lesbians, and me. Our boss was Randy, a hefty, grizzled dude. On breaks my coworkers would go outside to smoke pot behind the Dumpsters, and Randy would say, "Hold up! I'm coming too." They'd try to get me to come, but weed wasn't my thing. The place was a madhouse, basically. Everyone was always high, so food was constantly dropped onto the floor and then just thrown back into the fryer. "Doesn't matter. The grease burns the dirt off," was practically our motto. We horsed around all day. One time, I went to get biscuits, and one of my coworkers locked me in the freezer. Another time three coworkers cornered me and squirted a bunch of butter packets into my face. I actually get kind of nostalgic thinking about it. Hawthorne worked there with me for a while too, but of course he got fired.

· · ·

One day I was working the register, when I got a text from my mom. It was her birthday, and we had plans for the family to go out to Olive Garden that night.

I have the biggest news. It's going to change everyone's life, the text read.

What is it???

I'm not going to tell you. I'll tell you tonight at my party.

All day I wondered what this "big news" was. I worried she had plans to take Jake and me on some mini-vacation for the weekend. I'd been feeling down lately, fighting with Hawthorne a lot, and was not in the mood to take a road trip to Kansas City or wherever it might be. Finally evening came around, and I met my mom and Jake at the restaurant.

"Okay," I said as I sat down. "What's the big news? Are we going to Branson for the weekend?"

"Nope," said my mom. "I'm not telling until Derik gets here. Is Hawthorne coming?"

I'd invited Hawthorne, but he'd said he had plans with Ferris. I had my suspicions he was with Abby, though. I'd texted Ferris: *What are you and Hawthorne up to?* And he'd just texted back: *Hawthorne?*

"He's busy," I said.

Derik arrived, and we ordered calamari appetizers, plates of pasta, and a glass of white wine for Mom. Halfway through the dinner I tried again.

"Okay, Mom. Will you just tell us what this surprise is already?"

My mom took a deep breath. "Well . . . I was contacted today by a woman named Nancy McDonald who works as

a liaison at the Equality Center. She told me that an anonymous donor has offered to pay for your surgery."

My jaw dropped.

"Wait . . . what did you say?" I was scared that I had
misunderstood her. My throat felt like it had sunk into my
stomach.

"Your surgery is going to be covered," my mom said with
a giant grin. "An anonymous donor has followed your work
in the LGBT community and wants to help you. They're not
only offering to pay for the surgery, and all travel expenses
for you and me, but they're also offering to help sponsor you
through college."

I burst into tears in the middle of Olive Garden. And
then my mom started crying. A waiter came by to refill our
waters, but then scuttled away when he saw us sobbing.

"This is awesome!" said Derik. "I can't believe it!"

"It's amazing!" said Jake.

"I know!" I choked out in between cries. I pulled out my
phone and texted Hawthorne. *Someone just offered to pay for
my surgery!!!*

That's cool, he replied.

That's all he has to say? I thought. But I tried to not let his
reaction ruin the moment.

"We're going to try to schedule it for as soon as possible,
after you turn eighteen," my mom said.

My eighteenth birthday was six months away, which
suddenly felt like a lifetime.

"But who is this person?" I asked my mom. "I have to
thank them!"

"They want to remain anonymous," my mom said,

shrugging. "I suppose so they aren't solicited for money by others. . . . Trust me, it kills me too. I'm going to write a letter of thanks for Nancy McDonald to pass on. You should do the same."

"Of course," I said. My mind swam with images of who this mystery person could be, this person who was making it possible for me to finally feel whole.

Spring semester of my senior year began, and every day I counted down until May 13—the date I was scheduled to fly to California for my surgery, one day after my eighteenth birthday.

Meanwhile, things between my mom and Hawthorne got worse. He was supposed to have stayed only until the end of my junior year—his senior year—but then it had turned out he didn't have enough credits to graduate, and six months had turned into twelve. My mom got him a job as a cashier at Food Pyramid, where she worked in the pharmacy. They didn't even have an opening at the time, but my mom was so well liked at work that she convinced her boss to take Hawthorne on. She told Hawthorne, "I went out on a limb for you. Do not make me look like a fool." But after six weeks her boss came to her, saying that they had to let him go, that he was lazy and complaining to the customers about his job. My mom told Hawthorne to pack his stuff and get out.

Hawthorne called his grandpa, who gave him money to rent an apartment. Why he hadn't been able to do that two years before, when he'd first gotten kicked out of his mom's, was beyond my mom and me. He rented a small studio on

Memorial Avenue in Tulsa by the mall, and on March 1, Ferris and I helped him move in.

He didn't have much stuff—just a dirty red futon, his clothes, a few CDs, his computer, and a lamp and two chairs my mom had given him. We drove it all over to Memorial Avenue in the used car my mom and Dennis had chipped in to help Hawthorne buy. All through the move I could tell something was wrong. Hawthorne wasn't smiling, and whenever I'd joke or try to hug him, he'd ignore me. When all the stuff was in and Ferris was outside smoking, I lay down on the red futon.

"Hey, want to come here and relax with me?" I said.

"I'm gonna go smoke with Ferris," he said, heading out the door.

I had a sick feeling in my gut. I knew something bad was going to happen.

Hawthorne came back into the apartment with a scowl on his face. Ferris had gone home. I sat up on the red futon.

"Hawthorne, what's wrong?" I asked.

"Nothing. I'm fine," he said with an annoyed look.

"Are you sure? I can tell something's bothering you."

"No, there's nothing. I'm glad I got an apartment. I've got my own bathroom now!" He gave a cheap smile.

"Well, it's pretty late and there's school tomorrow, so I should get going," I said, getting up. I walked over and tried to give him a hug, but his body was stiff. He reeked of smoke. "Give me a call later and tell me how your new apartment is feeling, okay, hon?"

"Uh-huh," he said.

I drove home, and the next morning woke up to a

text from Hawthorne that took almost ten minutes to get through. In it, he told me that he was breaking up with me and that he was going to start dating Abby. He wrote that he loved her—that he always had—and that he wanted to be with her. For some reason, he felt compelled to tell me that she had come over the previous night and that they had had sex. He told me that I was a bitch, that I was always telling him what to do. He went so far as to write that he had only dated me so that he could have a place to live. He had used me and my mom.

I felt like my heart had stopped beating. I knew that Hawthorne had been horrible to me for the past six months and that really I should have been happy to be done with him, but I couldn't help it—he'd been my first love—and I was devastated. I tried not to cry, but the tears came anyway. I read the text one more time and then put the phone down. I couldn't breathe or see straight. I thought I would collapse onto the floor. But then, just as all my strength left me, I realized I hated him. And it was a strong, bitter hatred. After all I'd done, after all I'd sacrificed, *I* was the bad person? *No.* I imagined going back in time and breaking into the movie theater where Hawthorne had first kissed me. I'd have a gang of lipstick-wearing, walkie-talkie- and blackjack-wielding covert operatives with me. We'd bust in commando style and steal my past self away from him before I could fall in love.

I wiped the tears off my face, jumped up from my bed, and began manically getting dressed for school, all the while ripping photos of Hawthorne and me off the wall and throwing keepsakes into the trash. *Go to hell, Hawthorne,* I said to myself as I straightened my outfit in the mirror. Then I took a deep breath and walked into the kitchen for breakfast.

My mom was getting Jake ready for school, so I made myself a bowl of cereal and grabbed an orange from the fridge. I sat down on the living room couch and turned the TV on to *Buffy the Vampire Slayer*. I tried to ignore my feelings and focus on what I had to do for school—*I'm pretty sure the quiz will be easy today*—but then my mind would switch back to thoughts of Hawthorne—him and Abby having sex or giggling together over how stupid and easy to manipulate I am. And then the tears would start to come again.

"Baby, what's wrong?" my mom said, walking into the living room.

"Nothing. I'm fine. I'm just a little upset, but I'm okay." I tried not to look at her, because I knew if I did, I'd really start bawling.

My mom sat down on the other couch across from me. "Why?" she asked.

"Hawthorne broke up with me for Abby," I said. I looked away and wiped at my eyes with my fist.

"Oh . . ." My mom paused. "I'm sorry, honey, but that happens. And he was not good for you anyway. Trust me. This is a good thing."

"I know," I said. "I'm just upset that I stayed with him for so long. I kind of hate him."

"That's normal," my mom said with a chuckle. She got up and came and sat down on the couch next to me.

"First loves and first breakups are always hard," she said softly, rubbing my shoulder.

"Yeah," I said. Talking with my mom was really starting to make me feel a lot better.

"Now, I know this may seem too soon," she continued, "but I've been wanting to tell you. I was at OKEQ last week, meeting with Nancy McDonald about your surgery, and I saw the cutest trans boy—"

"Mom, what are you talking about?"

"He was there for a support group, and he was just the most adorable boy I have ever seen. If I were seventeen—"

"Mom! I've been single for, like, thirty minutes!" I said.

"I'm just saying," said my mom, lifting her hands up.

I rolled my eyes and grabbed my bag. "I've got to get to school."

A couple of weeks later Hawthorne had moved Ferris and three other friends into his studio apartment with him. I heard from mutual friends that all they did was lounge around, lighting candles, burning incense, and smoking cigarettes. One night I was on Facebook when a status update from Hawthorne popped up on my feed: "We've got a hundred candles going at once!" Followed shortly after by: "Shit! Fire!"

No one was hurt, but apparently Hawthorne and his friends had burned the apartment down. He would have to deal with that problem by himself now, though, or maybe Abby could console him. I, meanwhile, had just met a boy named Arin.

15

RAINBOW BEADS, CAP AND GOWN, AND A NEOVAGINA

It was April of my senior year. Nineteen days until surgery. I had been on several dates with Arin, the sweet transgender boy with gorgeous eyes I'd met at OKEQ. We still hadn't kissed, and it was driving me crazy. In just a few days that would change, though, at the 2012 Equality Gala.

The Equality Gala—where I was presented with the Carolyn Wagner Youth Leadership Award—was not only the night I first got together with Arin, but it was also an important night for my dad and me. A few days before the event, my mom told me my dad *might* come.

"He's been invited and he has a ticket, but we never know with your father," she said.

If my accepting an award in front of hundreds of people wasn't enough to pique my dad's interest in me, I honestly didn't know what would be.

"Great, good to know," I said with a deadpan tone. I refused to let his indifference hurt me anymore.

But as it turned out, he did show up. My mom, Jake,

Derik, and I drove over in a blue Hummer we'd borrowed for the evening, and when we arrived, there was my dad, looking a little lost and bewildered among the rainbow streamer decorations in the lobby of the convention center. I would find out later it was Jake who'd convinced him to go.

As we sat at our ballroom dining table, me anxiously trying to plan my acceptance speech, everyone else digging into the delicious food, I realized that this was the first time my whole family—Mom, Dad, Jake, Derik, and me—had been together in the same room in nine years.

"And now I'd like to introduce someone very dear to me, the recipient of the 2012 Carolyn Wagner Youth Leadership Award . . . ," Toby Jenkins was soon calling from the stage. And before I knew it, I was standing up there, staring out at a sea of faces. I'd given multiple speeches before, but this one was different—it was personal. Looking up at me now were all these people who had believed in me and supported me, some of whom I might not have been alive without. Dr. Laura Arrowsmith, Toby Jenkins, Dr. Brenda Bowman, Nancy McDonald, Arin and his family, and my family.

"I've come a long way in the past couple of years," I began. As I glanced down at my mom and dad—who had followed me to the front of the room and were standing just below the stage—I could see something in my dad's expression changing. "And we've come a long way as a community."

When I finished my speech and walked off the stage to a standing ovation, my dad was waiting for me. I'd noticed people in the audience crying but was honestly shocked to see my dad with tears in his eyes. I'd never seen him cry in my life.

"I'm so proud of you," he said.

"Thanks, Daddy," I said. I felt a swell in my heart.

My mom flung her arms around me. "You were amazing," she said.

My dad stepped in and gave me a hug too.

As the night turned to dancing and revelry, my dad proceeded to get properly smashed. He was a fun, good-spirited drunk that night, so I didn't mind. At one point I draped a bunch of rainbow beads around his neck.

"I'm so gay right now!" he said. "I love it!"

A slow song came on, and I noticed some of the girls dancing with their fathers.

"Do you want to dance, Daddy?" I asked.

"A father-daughter dance?" he said.

I nodded.

"It would be my honor," he said.

I leaned into his shoulder as we danced, the band playing "Moon River." I couldn't forgive him for everything, just like that, but in that moment I was able to love him again, and I felt loved back.

Eventually the night wound down and the crowd began to disperse. I'd invited Arin to spend the night, and he, my mom, Jake, Derik, my dad, and I all went out to the parking lot. I hugged my dad good-bye.

"Thanks for coming," my mom said to him.

"Thanks for making sure I did," he said.

Then Arin and I, giggly and flirty, hopped into the back of the Hummer, and we sped away from the gala.

A couple of weeks later, on May 10, 2012, I graduated from Bixby High School. The *Tulsa World* wanted to run a follow-up

piece on my graduating, so the entire day I was followed by a
camera crew.

Graduation is exciting, but it also involves a lot of waiting and standing around as the school attempts to organize
hundreds of students and the nearly one thousand friends
and family who have come to watch them. Our graduation
was held at the Mabee Center in Tulsa, and the first order
of business was getting changed into caps and gowns in the
crowded, hot changing rooms downstairs.

"This is it! We're finally leaving the hellhole that is Bixby
High!" said Skylar.

"Can you believe it?" I said.

I looked in the mirror and saw that my hair was completely frizzy and untamed. I was looking around to see if
anyone was using a comb, when my eyes fell on Catherine,
Maria, and Lisa standing in a group.

"Katie! Hi!" said Catherine, running over to me. She
flung her arms around my neck, bringing my entire body
down to her height.

"Hey, Catherine!" I said.

Maria and Lisa walked over too.

"You guys excited?" I asked.

"Hell yeah we are!" said Catherine.

"Yep!" said Maria.

"Oh yeah, so ready," said Lisa. She gave me a thumbs-up
sign but averted her eyes. Things were still awkward
between us.

A teacher came into the dressing room with a bullhorn.
She turned it on, and screeching feedback filled the room.
She adjusted the volume and began barking orders, giving us

complicated directions on where and when and how long to stand at various locations throughout the ceremony.

When we finally got up onto the stage, I repeated the directions over and over in my head. *Shake the principal's hand, receive diploma, shake her hand again, take a picture, walk forward, shake someone else's hand, walk forward again, shake another person's hand, take another picture, move across the stage and have your mortarboard tassel switched to the other side to represent having graduated.*

Hawthorne was supposed to graduate as well, but thankfully he'd decided not to come. He was the last person I felt like seeing. I looked out at the audience in the stands, searching for my family. Mom, Dad, Dennis, Derik, Jake, Grandma, and even Arin and his mom had all come to watch me. I saw Arin first, which made me blush and smile. As soon as he realized I was looking at him, he jumped up and began waving like a madman. He pointed with a finger, and I saw my mom waving and yelling herself. When she saw that I'd seen her, she put her hand to her waist as if to say, *It's about damn time you saw us!* Then she held up her camera, and I posed as she took a photo.

"Katie Rain Hill," the announcer called out. And soon I was moving flawlessly through all the steps. At the end of the stage, Mr. Flannery, a teacher who had always been kind to me, was there to switch my tassel.

"You look lovely today, Ms. Hill," he said. "Allow me to do the honors."

I was officially a high school graduate. Not only that, but I was the first openly transgender high school graduate in all of Oklahoma. In that moment the previous four years of hell and uncertainty were all worth it. I had stuck up for myself in the faces of those who hated me and wanted to hurt me, and I had won. In fewer than three years I had changed from a scared boy into a strong woman. The ability to be happy had been with me all along. All I'd had to do was trust and accept myself.

Two days after graduation, my eighteenth birthday arrived. My mom threw me a surgery/birthday party at OYP. There were balloons that said IT'S A GIRL! and there was a giant cake with "Happy Birthday, Baby Girl" written in icing. I'd told my mom I wanted a cake in the shape of a penis, so we could all take turns hacking a penis apart, but she thought that was too crude.

In attendance were Arin, of course, and all my friends from OYP—Brendan, Jess, Trina, Robbie, Jeanie, the new trans kid Brent, Andrea—as well as some of the kids at Bixby High I'd become closer to, like Adele, Stephanie, and Skylar. I'd invited Maria, but she couldn't make it, and Catherine was still off-limits. After Hawthorne and I had broken up, right before I'd met Arin, I'd briefly hooked up with this guy Michael, and I'd invited him to my party too, which did *not* please Arin. I'd begun to realize that Arin had a jealous streak in him—he hated seeing other guys pay attention to me. Michael and I were just friends at this point—and we'd hooked up only a couple of times—but as soon as he walked into the party, Arin was pissed.

"What is Michael doing here? Why'd you invite that creep?" he asked.

"He's my friend. Don't worry about it," I said. I gave

Arin a kiss. He looked especially cute in a red-and-yellow plaid button-down. "Just ignore him."

Arin seethed over Michael for a while, and Michael likewise fumed over Arin, but as it turned out, they had someone to hate more than each other: Hawthorne. Arin and Michael had both heard horror stories of how Hawthorne had treated me, so when Hawthorne and Abby walked into the party—*uninvited, mind you*—Arin and Michael switched their focus.

"I just saw Hawthorne walk in," said Michael, running up to Arin and me.

"No way," said Arin. "What the hell is he doing here?"

"I do not feel like seeing his face right now," I said. "I mean, I'm over it, but his face just pisses me off."

Hawthorne, with Abby, walked up to me.

"Hey, happy birthday," he said.

"What are you doing here?" I asked.

Michael and Arin stood on either side of me, glaring at him.

"Give us a minute?" Hawthorne said to Abby.

Abby flounced her ponytail and went off to eat my cake.

"Can I just talk to you outside?" Hawthorne asked me.

"No," I said. "Anything you have to say to me, I've already imagined you saying and dismissed. It's over."

"Please?" he asked. "This is really important. I just need to get this off my chest."

"Fine," I said.

"Are you okay?" Arin said to me, fists clenched at his side.

"Yeah, do you need us?" asked Michael, fists likewise clenched.

Arin and Michael looked at each other and nodded, apparently now best friends.

"I'll be fine," I said, and I walked with Hawthorne outside.

It was quiet in the night air of the parking lot, and I could hear the faint sounds of my party going on inside.

"Okay . . . ?" I prompted Hawthorne.

"I just wanted to say you look gorgeous tonight," said Hawthorne, "and I'm so happy for you that you're getting your surgery."

"Okay," I said, deadpan.

"Abby and I aren't exactly working out, and I think we're going to break up, and . . . I think you're an amazing person, and I would love the chance to date you again."

"Okay. Anything else?" I asked.

"Uh, no," said Hawthorne.

"Well, everything you just said I've already imagined you saying, and I'm not interested. There is literally nothing you can say to me that I want to hear, so I'd appreciate it if you'd take your skank girlfriend and get out of my party."

"I'm sorry," he said. "I hope we can stay friends, and maybe one day we'll be back together." Then he slunk away.

Five minutes later he and Abby were gone.

"Are you okay? Is everything fine?" Arin and Michael both said to me, coming up at once.

"Relax. Everything's perfect," I told them.

The party ended around midnight, and Arin came over to spend the night. We curled up on a pallet of blankets on the floor of my bedroom, alternating gossiping about the party and making out. Every now and then I'd remember—I'm leaving for my surgery tomorrow!—and would get a jolt of excitement.

"Do you want to try having sex again?" Arin asked.

"You mean the way we did it before?" I said.

A couple of weeks earlier Arin and I had tried having intercourse—as in penis-in-vagina sex—which had been a little weird, since in our case the penis was on a female and the vagina belonged to a boy. It had been a kind of virginity loss for both of us, and while it may not have been totally enjoyable, it had certainly brought us closer.

"Let's do it another way," I said now.

Afterward we cuddled for a while.

"Oh! I have something to give you," I said. I got up and rifled around in my closet. "Close your eyes."

Arin closed his eyes. I found what I was looking for and kneeled down in front of him.

"Okay, open," I said.

Arin opened his eyes, looked confused for a second, and then broke into a soft smile.

"Your 'hiding hoodie,'" he said.

I was holding my big, black, hooded sweatshirt. The one I'd worn nonstop for three years to hide my body.

"I want you to have it," I said.

We fell asleep on the floor, my hiding hoodie between us.

My alarm was set for seven a.m., and when I woke up, it felt like Christmas morning. Arin's mom, Denise, picked us up to drive my mom and me to the airport. At the Tulsa International Airport, Arin and I kissed good-bye.

"Text me as soon as you land," he said.

"I will," I said.

We thanked Denise, and then my mom and I grabbed our bags from the trunk and headed into the airport.

Waiting in the boarding area, I watched a YouTube video on my computer of Dr. Bowers performing a vaginoplasty. Maddie, from my trans support group at OKEQ, had sent it to me when I'd first talked about wanting to get surgery, and by now I'd seen the video dozens of times. As usual, I tried to ignore the comments at the bottom, where people felt the need to post things such as "Disgusting" and "It's a good thing doctors get paid 400K a year to do this" and "Only someone with a mental disorder would want this" and "I want to puke." I focused instead on the comments like "Can't wait . . . should have had it done years ago."

The video is up close and graphic. It's not for the squeamish, but I wanted to be fully aware of what was going to happen to my body. The video is only seven minutes long but covers what is typically a four-hour surgery. It takes you through the fifteen surgical steps:

- Harvest scrotal skin for neovaginal graft

- Orchiectomy (removal of the testicles)

- Catheterization of urethra

- Division of penile shaft into *corpus spongiosum* and *corpora cavernosa*

- Neoclitoris formation and creation of dorsal neurovascular pedicle

- Removal of erectile portions of *corpora cavernosa*

- Ligature placement of neoclitoris and dorsal neurovascular pedicle

- Creation of neovaginal cavity

- Creation of distal neovagina from scrotal skin

- Clearing of hair follicles from graft and attachment of vaginal graft to inverted penile skin

- Placement of graft-lined stint into final neovaginal location

- Creation of neourethra

- Creation of labia minora/clitoral hooding

- Drain placement

- Closure of labia majora

It's crazy impressive, is what it is. I haven't had too much personal experience with vaginas, but I showed post-op photos from Dr. Bowers' website to my lesbian friends, and they all agreed: "Looks like a real vagina to me!"

"We will now begin boarding flight 542 to San Carlos," the announcer called out.

I was so tired from staying up late with Arin that I fell straight to sleep on the plane. Honestly, I can fall asleep anywhere, anytime. I adore sleeping.

I woke up just as we landed. My mom and I rented a car and drove to our hotel in San Mateo, where we would be staying for twelve days. Dr. Bowers' office requires that you have a few days pre-op and a week post-op to rest and recover. At the hotel we lounged around watching TV while I waited for my presurgery meeting with Dr. Bowers. She was going to need to examine my genitals and make sure there wouldn't be any issues with the surgery.

At the hospital the nurse instructed me to take off all my clothes, put on a gown, and lie on the examining table with my feet in the stirrups. Because of my shame and alienation from my body, this was pretty much my nightmare scenario. The only people who had ever seen me naked were my mom, Hawthorne, and Arin. But I figured, *Dr. Bowers is going to have to see my penis eventually—spend four hours with it, in fact—so let's just do this.* I was lying there when the door creaked open and in walked Dr. Bowers, pushing her thin wire-frame glasses up on her nose.

"Oh! Hi . . . ," she said, as if she were surprised to see me there.

"Uh, hi," I said. There is nothing more awkward than greeting someone while your legs are in stirrups.

Dr. Bowers walked over and poked and prodded me a

little. *In just two days it won't be there anymore,* I told myself.

Dr. Bowers looked up and adjusted her glasses again. "Okay. . . . Well . . . everything seems good. . . . I guess I'll see you Wednesday," she said in a placid tone.

I liked her, and knew she was an amazing surgeon, but my God was she awkward.

"Um, okay. Thanks," I said.

And then, before I knew it, she had walked out the door.

That's it? I thought. I guess I'd assumed we'd chat a little more. At first I hadn't wanted her to come into the room, but now I kind of wished she'd stayed.

The day before my surgery I was allowed to consume only clear liquids, and after midnight, nothing. I also had to drink a bottle of this bowel prep stuff to clear my system out, and that kept me in the bathroom, as sick as hell, for hours.

"You're sure you're okay?" my mom shouted from our hotel room bed.

"I'm fine. I'm just dying," I shouted back, hunched over the toilet.

I woke up the next morning, giddy and nervous. I knew this was a major very invasive surgery, and that a lot could potentially go wrong. I could bleed to death. I could react badly to the anesthesia and not wake up. My nerves could be damaged and I could lose all sensation in my new vagina. Honestly, though, I wasn't that worried. I'd thoroughly researched Dr. Bowers. She'd performed this surgery hundreds of times, and I felt confident. When we'd first scheduled the surgery and I'd spoken with her on the phone, she'd told me that because I was young, I had a very high chance of retaining all sexual feeling. No part of me second-guessed my decision to have surgery, even for a moment. I wanted this more than anything else, and it was finally, finally happening.

"You ready?" my mom asked, standing by the door. I could tell that she was nervous.

"I'm gonna be fine, Mom," I said.

"I know you are, baby," she said.

She drove me over to the hospital while I watched the YouTube surgery video one more time on my phone. Egad, it certainly was graphic. But, yes, I was *ready*.

The days following my surgery are foggy. It's remarkable that I can remember anything at all, I was so doped up on morphine. What I mainly remember, though, is an overwhelming feeling of relief and anticipation. I couldn't wait to be strong again and move around in my new body. The nurse told me that, at first, walking would be difficult. Not just because of the pain but because your body has to learn to realign itself with the new genital arrangement. I had to stay in my hospital bed for forty-eight hours and then move to a hospital residence inn for the rest of the week. Every day Arin Skyped me.

"I miss you. How are you?" he'd ask, looking nervous.

"Okay," I'd manage to whisper. It was comforting to have his sweet, smiling face on my laptop, though I was so out of it on painkillers, I had trouble keeping up a conversation.

On the second day I felt good enough to get out of bed and try walking—but as soon as my feet hit the floor, the rest of me did too. My mom and the nurse had to come pull me up, all my wires and drain tubes in a tangle.

On the third day my mom and I moved to the residence inn. As soon as we got there, I hobbled into the bathroom, stripped off all my clothes, and stared at myself in the full-length mirror. When I saw my body, I started crying. They were tears of joy. Sure, my vagina looked like an obscenely swollen red wound packed with gauze and hospital tape. But it was a *vagina*. *I'm finally done with that nonsense,* I thought.

I got back to Oklahoma on May 25, and the next day Arin invited me to go out on his boat with his family. I was still in so much pain, but going on a boat meant I got to wear a bikini, right? So, *hell yeah*.

Arin had given me one of his old swimsuits—a little white bikini. Slipping it on felt amazing. Whenever I used to go swimming or to water parks, I would have to duct tape my genitals up to try to hide them, and even then I still had to wear bikini bottoms with little skirts. It was hugely uncomfortable and impossible to have fun. I'd spend the whole time anxious that someone would notice my bulge. Now, finally, I felt right.

Of course, my vagina had still only just begun to heal. Out on Arin's boat, I had to carry around a little inflatable doughnut to use every time I sat down. Whenever the motor was going, I'd bounce up and down on my doughnut and feel like my vagina was going to get ripped in half. Well, ripped in half again. It was a lot of fun, though. In the photos I have from that trip, everyone has these huge smiles on their faces—except, my huge smile is also a grimace of pain.

• • •

Arin and I did exciting things all summer while I was recovering. We went rock climbing, did archery, took road trips to Missouri and Kansas, played laser tag, went hiking and camping. We did everything we could think of.

One night after a full day of goofing off at the lake, we went back to Arin's house.

"Dinner's in half an hour," Denise called as we ran up the stairs to his bedroom. I went into the bathroom and changed out of my bikini and into clothes.

"Hey, Arin," I said, walking into his bedroom and tossing the bikini onto the bed. "Want to try this on?"

"What? No way!" he said.

"I totally get it if you don't want to," I said. "I just thought it would be silly. You can draw a mascara mustache on me if you want."

The more comfortable I was in my own gender, the more I found myself wanting to play around with it. I went over to his mirror and began to apply the mascara mustache myself. Arin stood next to me and examined his facial hair. He'd been on T for a few months now, and his hair was coming in nicely (exactly as I'd predicted). He was feeling a lot more confident in his looks too.

"Eh, why not? Give me that bikini," he said. He went over to the bed, stripped off his clothes, and put the bikini on. He turned around. "Well, what do you think?"

"You look gorgeous," I said.

"What? I look as manly as hell," he said. He flexed his biceps, and we both started laughing.

He took the bikini off and pulled his shorts and tank top back on.

I walked over, and we started kissing, tickling, and wrestling.

"My mom's gonna call us for dinner any minute!" he said.

"So?" I said, and we toppled onto his bed, laughing and making out. We lay there and looked into each other's eyes for a moment.

"I love you," we said, for the first time, at the same time.

We both immediately started giggling.

"I can't believe that just happened," I said.

Later that night we got a ladder, climbed onto the roof of his house, and just sat there, cuddling and watching the stars for more than an hour.

When I found out my donor was offering to pay not only for my surgery but also for four years of college (as long as I maintained a 3.0 GPA), I immediately started researching potential colleges. I visited a school in Chicago, which I liked, but the idea of moving so far away from home made me anxious. I decided, for now, I wanted to stay close to my mom and friends.

Of the colleges in Oklahoma, my top choice was the University of Tulsa, one of the most prestigious colleges in the southwestern states. When I took a tour, I loved how perfectly kept the sprawling grounds were. The tour guide pointed out that all the prim trees lining the pathways were genetically identical. The arborists had started with the DNA of one tree, and the rest were clones. I applied that winter and was accepted to TU's graduating class of 2016.

At the beginning of my freshman year of college, I did another follow-up interview with *Tulsa World*. The original article had focused on my relationship with Hawthorne, and this time when they asked about dating, I told them about Arin.

"And how does he accept your being trans?" they asked.

"Pretty well, considering he's trans too," I said.

The follow-up article ran, and the very same day I received a call from a media content company in London called Barcroft, wanting to represent Arin and me.

"Individually you guys are great . . . but together you're phenomenal," the Barcroft representative said. "And we can make you huge. You're only local now, but we want to bring your story worldwide."

My mom and Arin's mom, Denise, got on the phone with the people at Barcroft. Our mothers told the company they wanted to be certain that whatever media attention came, Arin and I wouldn't be made fun of. There could be no *Jerry Springer Show* or anything like that. Barcroft assured my mom and Denise that that wouldn't happen. Their goal was for Arin and me to help educate people and . . . also eventually get a Lifetime movie and become rich. A Lifetime movie sounded like a pipe dream, but Arin and I did want the opportunity to tell our stories and help people. The contract was for only a year, so we figured there wasn't any harm in trying it.

The first TV interview Arin and I did after signing with Barcroft was *Inside Edition*. The film crew came to Arin's house and set up lights and equipment in his living room. They asked us questions about our childhoods and our feelings for each other. We were jittery and excited, giggling at each other during the breaks. The segment aired in October of my freshman year of college, and after that, people wouldn't leave us alone. The phone was ringing off the hook, and more and more interviews were booked.

It was fun having all the attention, and it was thrilling to see myself on TV. But it was also unsettling. Every media outlet wanted to hear about how in love Arin and I were and how we were perfect for each other. The truth was, ever since I'd started college, I'd found myself feeling more distant from him. He didn't understand the pressures of a college workload, and I began to feel like everything in our relationship revolved around what he wanted to do. He rarely came to visit me at my dorm on the TU campus, and instead always wanted me to drive back to Broken Arrow to hang out with him at his house. Meanwhile, I was having fun getting to know my new group of friends— Mark, Jessica, Liz, Justin, Jon . . . and especially Billy. I was so excited about my brand-new life at college and just wanted to feel independent. I really loved Arin, but I kept wondering if maybe we'd be better as just friends. How do you break up, though, when all of a sudden it feels like the whole world is rooting for your relationship? Arin and I were getting media attention *because* we were a couple. This was a big chance to spread the word about transgenderism, be an advocate, and help people. I didn't want to let that go.

Another opportunity for advocacy came in January, when Toby Jenkins invited me to go to the Creating Change conference, one of the largest annual gatherings of activists, organizers, and leaders in the LGBT movement in the US. It was over the weekend, so I would have to miss only two days of school. Toby Jenkins, Mary Jones—the OKEQ program coordinator—some other teens, and I drove sixteen hours down to Atlanta together to attend.

I was excited. It was my first big conference, and I imagined groups of like-minded people sitting down to learn and then coming together to contemplate how we could make our mutual goals easier to obtain.

Good Lord was I wrong.

Instead it was a crack ton of people with so many different ideals in one room that nothing could get done. One of the first sessions I went to was supposed to be on LGBT rights in schools. It was a one-hour session, and the first thirty minutes were taken up by one woman crying and bitching because there wasn't a recycling bin in the room.

"I am not going to just throw away my trash!" she announced to the presenters at the podium and a room full of forty people, sitting there waiting. She refused to let them begin until a recycling bin was delivered to the room.

When the lecture finally started, the next thirty minutes were taken up by bickering. The Q&A portion was supposed to be at the end, but people shouted their opinions out in the middle of the talk.

"I think it's outrageous that trans people expect to have access to any bathroom they choose."

"Are you crazy? Of course trans people should have access to their desired bathroom!"

"Well, you're stupid, because it's going to cause riots in schools, and gay kids will get a bad name."

The session was supposed to be about a variety of LGBT

rights in schools, not just toilet privileges for trans people. But the lecturer never got past the third slide.

There were booklets with all the different sessions listed, and Toby wanted us to attend as many as possible. One session was a general discussion group exclusively for trans people. I thought that seemed cool, so I signed up.

A cameraman had met me at the conference to follow me around, because Barcroft wanted to do a segment on me at Creating Change. What the cameraman ended up filming at the trans discussion group was—he later told me—so horrible, it made him cry. "I could never, ever show this on television," he said.

When I arrived at the session, I let everyone know that I was being filmed for TV and said that if anyone didn't want to be seen, to let the cameraman know. A couple of people said they didn't and moved so their backs were facing the camera.

Another woman announced that she was a transgender porn star and that after the group she would be showing a promo of her new porn film in her apartment if anyone wanted to join. I thought that seemed a little inappropriate, but whatever.

We started the discussion, and the first ten minutes went fine. I threw out some opinions; other people tossed out theirs. This time when we discussed bathroom rights, everyone agreed. Then one girl—a female-born person who presented as masculine and identified as androgynous but preferred female pronouns—began talking about how she only likes to have sex with trans men.

"It's the only way I can orgasm," she said. "I'd like to

be with a woman, but I'm really only able to enjoy sex with trans men. I don't know why."

Everyone shared their opinions, and I said, "It may be that trans men share a similar experience with you and it's a mental-emotional thing. We're all born either a boy or a girl, and then we transition into our appropriate desired gender. Maybe you feel connected to trans men because you've both experienced being ridiculed as women and having masculine tendencies, or you share similar ideologies or cognitions. I'm trans and I like dating cisgender men, but I have a boyfriend right now who's trans, and he understands me better than anybody else. Maybe it's similar for you, and you're sexually drawn to that."

The entire room exploded.

"Excuse me, *bitch*. I was not born a boy. I was born a *baby*," the porn star woman said.

"You're born either male or female," I tried to explain. "I'm not putting that on people; society is putting that on people."

Everyone continued yelling.

"When the doctor pulls you out, they call you a boy or a girl," I said. "I was born biologically a boy, but I was always a full woman."

"Excuse me, but you need to shut your mouth," an older trans man said to me. "Because everyone here is pissed off at what you're saying."

The group moderators, who had told us at the beginning that all opinions were welcome and that any disagreement would be handled with polite rebuttal, just sat there while everyone kept screaming at me. It was as if I were some cisgender hussy who didn't know what she was talking about, trying to tell them what was what.

The session ended, and I went straight to my hotel room, where I fell onto my bed and sobbed. Negative thoughts filled my head.

My new friends at TU had stopped talking to me a few months earlier. Being rejected by them had made me feel like no one in the cisgender community understood me. Now it felt like no one in the LGBT community understood me either.

I went and knocked on Toby's hotel room door to see if he was there. He let me in, and I sat down in his chair.

"Toby," I said, "I don't know if you know this, but the LGBT community is *fucked up*. We're not a community. We're a bunch of people who think we belong together, who think we can relate to one another, but who really just hate one another and are out to destroy one another."

Toby lowered his head. "Katie," he said softly.

I felt horrible that I had disappointed him.

But then he looked up. "I've taken a lot of kids on this trip, and so many of them have had terrible experiences, but you're the only one who's been able to express why." Toby shifted into his booming preacher voice. "But you know what, Katie? Let me tell you something. This messed-up stuff? This is *all* we have. The conflict going on in these rooms right now is actually the greatest thing that could happen, because conflict bears results. When a bunch of people bicker and complain, eventually they come to conclusions about what we need to do next. It's because of this chaos that we're getting as far as we are today."

What he said eventually made sense. But at the time I was still angry. "That's stupid," I said.

I lay awake that night, trying to figure out what I had said in the trans discussion group that everyone had found so offensive. Maybe I should have just used the phrase "socialized as a boy" rather than "born as a boy." But honestly, that seemed like touchy semantics to me. Whether we like it or not, we're all assigned a sex at birth. The doctor announces, "It's a boy!" or "It's a girl!" and there's nothing any of us can do about it. Didn't the other trans people know that that was all I meant?

I thought about everything I'd learned in the previous few years as I'd come to understand the intricacies of trans theory and rhetoric. Through conversations with other queer people and by reading anything I could find on the Internet, I had a pretty in-depth understanding of gender. I know that sex, gender identity, gender expression, romantic attraction, and sexual attraction are all different things, independent of one another and each with their own continuum. "Biological sex" refers to your organs, chromosomes, and hormones, and ranges from male to female, with intersex in between. Gender identity is how you think about yourself, and ranges from man to woman, with genderqueer in between. Gender expression is how you present yourself using behavior and dress, and ranges from masculine to feminine, with androgynous in between. "Romantic attraction" relates to who you are emotionally attracted to, and "sexual attraction" relates to who you are physically attracted to. Both of these range from heterosexual to homosexual, with bisexual in between. You can also be agendered or asexual. All the myriad options from these various spectrums are legitimate and should be respected. But right now, with our society as it is, many of these variations are still looked on with suspicion.

The people in the trans discussion group may not like that they were assigned a gender at birth, but for the foreseeable future that's what happens when you're born. I wish I could have a child and give them a neutral gender, but that's not an option. That child will look at society and be overwhelmed by what their socialization should be. Even if you're not socializing your kid, the rest of the world is, and the child is going to look to you for guidance.

On the way back to Oklahoma, I sat up front while Mary Jones drove. She's an amazing woman, and I know she's got my back. I told Mary how I'd been attacked during the trans discussion group.

"You know, Katie," she said, "not all queer people are saints. Like the rest of the world, a lot of us are plum crazy. You've just got to find the people you like and relate to and be grateful for them."

I looked around the car at Mary, Toby, and Robbie and Trina zoning out on their iPods.

"I am," I said.

Arin understood so much about me. But one thing he never got, no matter how hard I tried to drill it into him, is how truly competitive I am. Maybe it's because of my years excelling at school when that was the only thing I had, or maybe it's in my DNA, but I cannot stand to lose.

In March of my freshman year at TU, Arin invited me to go skiing with him and his family. We were lying in bed in my dorm room one of the few times he'd come to see me.

"But I've never skied before," I said. "I won't be good at it."

"So what? It will be fun. Besides, it's more than just skiing. Hot cocoa, snuggling by the fire . . ." He wrapped his arms around me and nuzzled his nose into my cheek. I shifted away from him.

"Arin, I know your family and you guys love skiing. It's mainly going to be skiing. I'll have an inferiority complex. I can't help it, and I don't want to be this way, but I know for a fact that if I'm not good at skiing—which I won't be—I'm going to get upset, and no one will have a good time."

He looked genuinely confused.

"That's crazy. You don't have to be good at it to have fun! Come on!"

I was starting to feel a little smothered in the bed next to him. I got up to get a glass of water. "I also don't like the cold, and I have a shit ton of schoolwork I need to catch up on. I don't want to go," I said.

Arin sat up and looked at me with this puppy-dog expression I was beginning to grow more and more weary of. *Why can't this boy ever accept no for an answer?*

"We never do anything together anymore!" he said. "I feel like you don't even care about me. All I want is for you to come skiing! Why is that so hard? Why can't you just—"

"Fine! I'll come," I snapped. I drank my water, got back into bed, and turned out the light.

Arin scooted close and put his arm around me. "I love you," he said.

"I love you, too," I said quietly back. But inside my head I thought, *This relationship is over.*

The trip was a disaster. During the car ride to Copper Mountain in Colorado, Arin; his mom; his chatterbox little brother, Wesley; and Arin's friends Tim and Jamie were all laughing, talking, and playing music, while I sat in the back with my philosophy, anthropology, and English textbooks, desperately trying to study. Arin thought homework was just homework, the worksheet you dash off before second period. He had no concept of what college, especially a rigorous college like TU, was like. Doing well was not only personally important, but it was also imperative if I wanted my donor to continue funding me.

Out on the slopes I was miserable. Everyone else had skied before, and even though I like to think I pick things up quickly, I couldn't get a handle on it. Every couple of feet I fell over, and everyone would giggle and say, "Come on, Katie. You can do it!" Their voices sounded patronizing, and I could tell they were all annoyed with me for slowing them down. I hated being locked into the awkward long skis, I hated my stifling puffy snowsuit, and I hated the freezing snow trapped inside it from all the times I'd fallen over. At one point I started crying.

"Katie, what is *wrong*?" asked Denise.

"I've never skied before!" I sobbed, really blubbering now. "Arin, I *told* you I wouldn't like this."

"Jesus," Jamie said to Tim. I watched them exchange snotty looks.

"How about just you and I take a ride up the ski lift together, okay?" asked Arin. He looked really upset.

"I guess . . . ," I said.

"You guys, we'll meet up with you later," he shouted to the others.

I appreciated his trying to take the time out to be with me, but honestly, all I kept thinking was, *I never should have agreed to come.*

We rode the ski lift to the top of the mountain, and I'll admit, the view was breathtaking—hills of smooth, sparkling snow for miles, under a crisp blue sky. When we reached the top, he pulled out a tungsten ring.

No, I thought, my heart sinking.

"I wanted to give you this on top of a mountain," he said. "I love you, and I want you to know that I will always be there for you. This is a promise ring."

I let him slip the ring over my finger, but inside I felt terrible. I didn't want to be in the relationship anymore. But what could I do? How could I end things on top of this majestic mountain, with this expensive ring, and with that expression on his face?

"Thank you," I said. And we kissed. But all I felt was deadness inside.

On the way back down the mountain I took an especially bad fall and twisted my ankle.

"I can't do this anymore!" I said to Arin, angry and in pain.

"Are you really hurt?" he asked.

"Yes!"

"I'll take you back to the cabin," he said.

At least I can get some studying done now, I thought.

Arin helped me to the cabin, gave me a quick kiss, and then ran off to rejoin his family and friends. They didn't return until evening.

The next day they all wanted to go skiing. Since my ankle was still sore, I was once again left in the cabin.

So, after not even wanting to go on the trip at all, I was segregated from the group to spend the week in an uncomfortable cabin by myself. I tried to focus on studying but realized I'd left some of my most important books and papers at home. There wasn't even Internet access.

On the drive back Arin tried to get me to say what I'd liked about the trip. I told him, "Frankly, nothing."

Denise laid into me. "Katie! I spent a lot of money driving you kids up here, and I'd like a little gratitude instead of just complaining."

I sank into my seat.

When we got back to Arin's house, he and I went into his room. He sat on his bed and tried to pull me down next to him. He had a hopeful smile, like making out on his bed would make everything okay. I stood back, my arms folded around me. I stared around his room—his weights in the corner, his giant white peace symbol and GAY ST. street sign nailed to the wall—this place that had always made me feel so happy and comfortable. I looked back at him.

"I want to break up," I said. I took the promise ring off my finger and tried to hand it back to him.

"What?" The word barely passed his lips. He looked down at the promise ring as if he couldn't believe I was giving it back to him.

"It's always just about what you want to do. You never listen to what I need." I started crying.

Arin started bawling too. "I'm sorry! I shouldn't have made you come. I'll change. I'll be better."

Denise poked her head in the door. "Is everything okay in here?" she asked.

"Katie wants to break up," said Arin in between sobs.

Denise glared at me.

"I love you," I said to Arin, still crying. "I just can't do this anymore."

"You obviously don't love him, because you're doing this to him," Denise said.

"Mom, can you just give us a minute?" asked Arin.

Denise shut the door.

"Please," he said to me. "I swear I'll be better."

I loved Arin and didn't want to lose him. "Okay . . . ," I said.

I let him slip the promise ring back on, but once again instead of feeling happy, I just felt anxious. *We're only teenagers,* I thought. *But he's treating our relationship as if we're going to be together forever.* Your teens and twenties are supposed to be a time of experimentation and meeting and dating new people, aren't they? The truth was, I wanted to try dating other guys. And I didn't know it at the time, but I was about to meet one.

I've always been fascinated by anthropology, and during second semester of my freshman year, I signed up for an anthropology class called Magic, Witchcraft, and Religion. Topics included shamanism, sorcery, ritual and symbol, rites of passage, and cult movements, with an emphasis on the diversity of beliefs and practices and their possible functions in human societies. I loved it.

One day I was walking to class when I heard a voice right behind me.

"Wait! Katie, wait up!"

I turned around, and this guy from class was running to catch up with me. I recognized him, but I didn't know how he knew my name.

"I'm gonna walk with you to class," he said. "I don't wanna walk in after you, because you're always the latest, so if I'm after you, then I'm *really* late."

"Ha," I said. But I let him walk with me.

"I'm Todd, by the way."

As soon as we reached the classroom door, Todd cut right in front of me and went in first. *Asshole!* But it was kind of funny.

After class Todd came up to me.

"You know, you're pretty cool. Why don't we get something to eat?" he said.

Arin and I had agreed to stay together, but this was just lunch, right? Harmless. And besides, I wasn't even sure what I thought of this Todd guy.

We went to Brownies, this old-style diner with a soda counter where you can order hamburgers, chili dogs, homemade root beer, and every kind of pie—from coconut cream to peach to peanut butter chocolate.

As soon as we walked in, the Chordettes' "Mr. Sandman" began playing, and we both started singing along. I was shocked he knew it. I'd gotten Arin into 1950s music too, but I'd never met another person my age who liked it on their own. We sat at the counter, ordered burgers and chili fries, and bonded over loving old-time bands. As we chatted, I surveyed Todd. He was cute, but I wasn't really attracted to him. He had a handsome face and all, but his hair was ridiculous. It was like a giant, fluffy brown helmet.

"Do you ever cut your hair?" I asked.

"Don't even mention cutting my hair," he said. "My hair is me."

What an amusing character. I shall call him Sir Periwinkle. I know, random.

"What are you thinking?" he asked, grinning at me. "You've got this weird, sly look on your face like I shouldn't trust you."

"Maybe you shouldn't," I said with a smile, and I took a long sip of root beer.

That night my friend Alexis, also from Magic, Witchcraft, and Religion, asked if I wanted to hang out. Alexis is pretty quiet but also really fun and into nerdy things like me. We made plans to go see *Iron Man 3*, and she asked, "Hey, can my friend Todd come?"

"You mean big-hair Todd from class? Sure. I just had lunch with him today."

I think Alexis had an idea that Todd liked me, because the whole evening she kept trying to get us to sit near each other. At the movie theater she stopped before sitting down next to me.

"Todd, do you want to sit next to Katie?" she asked.

Todd shrugged. "Sure," he said.

After the movie, when we all went out to eat at a diner, she did it again. "Todd, you can squeeze in next to Katie," she said.

I tried to give Alexis a look like, *What are you doing?* But she ignored me.

Afterward, when we walked back to her car, she said, "Todd, do you want to sit in the back with Katie?"

"Okay!" said Todd.

At this point I was feeling pretty awkward, sitting in the back with Todd while Alexis drove up front.

"So," said Todd, turning to me, "are you single? 'Cause I'm just wondering whether I should turn on 'the Todd charm' or not."

"'The Todd charm,'" I said, laughing. I have to admit I was a bit curious about this supposed Todd charm.

"I'm not single," I said. "But I am having complications in my relationship. . . ."

"Okay," said Todd, nodding. Then we both looked out the window.

One of the complications in my relationship with Arin—in addition to him not understanding the demands of college life—was sex. We were emotionally connected, and he was hands-down the hottest guy I'd ever been with, but we struggled with the physical intimacy. The first couple of weeks we were dating, we couldn't get enough of each other, and even though we were both dysphoric about our bodies, we worked through those feelings and were intimate in all the various ways most couples put their bodies together. But after my surgery, something changed between us. For one, my vagina was out of action for a long time as I recovered. It was more than that, though, because even after I was all healed up and ready to use my vagina, I didn't feel the same hunger for him. When we did have sex, I often felt like he only focused on what felt good for him. A lot of nights, we would end up just cuddling and falling asleep.

In May of 2013, Arin went to Cleveland for his top surgery. Some trans men need to have double mastectomies in order to have a flat chest, but because Arin's breasts were small, he was able to have keyhole surgery and liposuction of his breasts, a much less invasive procedure. Before he left, he gave me his ratty, black "hiding hoodie" just as I had given him mine.

Shortly after he came back, Barcroft shot a segment on us for German television. They wanted to film me driving over to Arin's house and then pretending to see his chest postsurgery for the first time.

"Tell us how *worried* you were while he was having surgery," the interviewer said as we drove to Arin's house, a little microphone clipped to the collar of my blue V-neck shirt.

"Yeah, I was worried . . . ," I said. But truthfully, I hadn't been worried at all. He'd had an extremely low-risk surgery with one of the best surgeons in the country. Unless there had been some freak accident, I had known he was going to be fine.

"Were you afraid he was going to *die?*" the interviewer prompted.

"Not really," I said.

I parked outside Arin's house, and we did our whole fake reunion and revealing of the postsurgery chest (which in reality I'd already seen a bunch of times).

"Oh, wow . . . ," I said as they instructed me to run my finger over his nipples. Next, per usual, they wanted us to get into bathing suits and go out on Arin's boat.

"Tell us how you couldn't live without Arin," the interviewer said as I awkwardly sat on Arin's lap in the boat.

"But . . . I could live without him," I said.

Arin looked at me, hurt. "What?"

"Come on. We're teenagers who have been dating for a year and a half. We're not gonna kill ourselves if we break up," I said. What I was thinking was, *And I kind of want to break up right now. If all these people weren't here,* that's *what we'd be talking about.*

"Well, I couldn't live without you," said Arin. "I don't know what I'd do."

After the interview, Arin asked if I wanted to stay for dinner, but I decided to go home. Being around his family only added to the pressure to feel happy with him. After a day of talking about how in love we were, I just wanted to be alone.

Driving back to campus, my brain was churning with conflicting thoughts. I was so sick of the journalists trying to manufacture a romantic story for their viewers when I was feeling pretty much the opposite of romantic toward Arin. But then, I was incredibly grateful to Barcroft for creating all these opportunities for us to share our story. Still, why did it always have to be about the romance between me and Arin? The while thing was starting to feel so false.

The truth is, as excited as I was for Arin to finally have the body—at least on top—that he'd wanted for so long, I actually kind of missed his breasts. I had liked them because they'd symbolized that he, like me, was trans. Of course, he was still trans after surgery, but I missed having such a prominent reminder that he was like me. This may sound confusing, since I too had had surgery and for all intents and purposes now had a female body, but despite my surgery, I still experienced moments of body dysphoria, where I felt I looked like a man. Maybe that's just the way the trans brain works—you can never fully escape the anxiety that you're in the wrong body. After his surgery Arin no longer looked the way I felt inside, so I missed his old chest. One night we talked about it, and Arin told me he felt the same way about my losing my penis.

Arin and I continued to try to make things work, but the fact was that my heart wasn't in it, and hadn't been for quite some time. My freshman year ended, and summer began. Todd was moving into a house just off campus with some TU friends, and I spent the next few weeks helping them move furniture in and paint the walls. The more I hung out with Todd, the more I liked him. I discovered that we shared a lot of the same ideals—he was accepting of gay people and overall an open-minded guy. He was also kind and always happy to listen and talk when I was feeling down. I ended up telling him about some of the relationship troubles I was having with Arin. Todd didn't know that Arin and I were trans, and I felt no need to tell him.

One night after a full day of painting, a bunch of us sat around the house playing Arkham Horror, a board game based on the work of H. P. Lovecraft. The game went on for hours, and we were all pretty tired of it by the end. Everyone got up to leave, and our friend Mac asked Todd if he could drive him back to TU.

"Hey, Katie," Todd said. "After I drop Mac off, do you want to keep hanging out and play video games?"

"Sure," I said.

We drove Mac home and then went back to the house. It was just Todd and me. I realized I felt kind of nervous. But why? I liked Todd only as a friend, right? The house was sparse, just a few random items of furniture scattered around, the smell of paint still fresh on the walls. We played Super Smash Bros. for Wii on cushions in the living room for a while and then wound up in the largest bedroom in the house, which was empty save for a pile of pillows. Todd threw one at me.

"Dick," I said. And threw one back.

There was a brief but energetic pillow fight, and then we fell to the ground, a pillow between us. We could see stars out of the window and started talking about the universe, the meaning of life, and nonsense like that.

Then Todd leaned in and kissed me.

As soon as Todd kissed me, I realized, *I really, really like this guy.* But at the same time I was thinking, *I'm with Arin. This is bad. Just get up and leave right now.*

"Are you okay?" asked Todd, looking at me with a nervous smile.

"Yeah," I said, but my mind was racing. *You're miserable with Arin. Neither of you are happy, even if you're the only one who admits it. And here's this guy who makes you feel good, who does make you happy.*

Todd leaned in and tried to kiss me again. I knew what I was doing was wrong, but in the moment I just couldn't help myself. I put my arms around him and kissed him back.

Todd rolled on top of me, putting his hands all over my body. It felt so good. He started to take off my clothes, and I could feel myself getting really turned on. It was as if nothing could stop this. He took off my pants, and I thought, *Are we actually doing this? Am I ready? Yes.*

We started having sex, and it was the sex I'd been waiting years to be able to have, the sex I had fantasized about for so long and that for so long had seemed an impossible wish. It was finally actually happening, and it felt amazing.

Todd and I never went to sleep that night. We stayed up until eight in the morning talking and then went to Waffle

House for breakfast. We ate the morning special and listened to Katy Perry's "Teenage Dream" on the jukebox. On the drive back from Waffle House, Todd turned to me.

"Will you be my girlfriend?" he asked.

"I . . . need to think about things," I said. "I need to figure out stuff with Arin."

"You do?" said Todd, with a disturbed look on his face. "I thought you and Arin were broken up."

"Oh, no, not exactly," I said. I looked out the window and bit my lip. I had to admit to myself that the way I'd talked about my relationship with Arin to Todd, it was understandable that he'd assumed we were actually over.

"Well . . . to be completely honest, we're not officially broken up."

"Wow," said Todd. There was an almost sarcastic tone to his voice. "That's good to know now."

"Would that have stopped you from doing what we did last night?" I asked.

Todd's face softened. "No," he said.

"I just need some time to figure things out, okay?" I said.

Todd nodded and stared back out at the road. I could tell from his eyes how hurt he was.

A few days later Todd left for a vacation in Russia for three weeks. I spent the time trying to process my feelings. I loved Arin, and I felt connected to him in ways I knew I never could with anyone else, but I wasn't happy dating him. I felt like the whole world expected us to be together. Here we were, two trans kids in Oklahoma who had, against all odds, found each other and fallen in love. Yes, it's an amazing story, and I feel so lucky to have met

Arin, but it was as if everyone's own hopes and dreams for finding love were somehow pinned on us. I just couldn't do it anymore.

"I want to break up," I told Arin. We were sitting on his bed.

He started crying and immediately recited what he always said: that he'd change, that he'd be better.

"I'm serious. We're not happy together," I said. It killed me seeing him in so much pain.

"Is it someone else?" he said in a wavering voice. "That Todd guy?"

He knew I'd been spending a fair amount of time helping out at Todd's new house.

"It's not someone else," I said. Guilt bit into my insides. I hated lying to Arin, but I couldn't stand the thought of hurting him any more than I already was. And besides, it wasn't as if Todd and I were officially dating— we'd just had that one indiscretion. *Maybe I'll even break it off with Todd*, I thought. What I'd done with Todd was greedy and impulsive and just the thought of him now filled me with shame. Yes, I affirmed to myself, I'll break things off with Todd. I barely knew Todd, and here was Arin, whom I *did* know and who knew me better than anyone else. I had gone into this conversation determined to end things with Arin, but now, staring into his sweet, loving eyes, I found myself wondering if there were actually a way we could make things work.

Arin put his head in his hands. "It's just . . . I'll do anything to keep you," he said. "I love you so much."

"I love you, too . . . ," I said.

"So we can try to make it work? You'll give me another chance?"

"Yes," I said. But as soon as I said it, I knew I had made a mistake.

As the horrible paradox that is the human condition goes, as soon as I agreed to stay with Arin, the feelings of shame I'd had around Todd were replaced with an irresistible crush. Todd returned from Russia and called to invite me over to his parents' house in Broken Arrow. Hearing his voice on the phone, I felt my whole body flutter. I know I should have been up-front with Todd and told him I had chosen Arin, but instead I kept things vague.

"So did you think things over while I was gone?" Todd asked. "Will you be my girlfriend?"

"I'm kind of still figuring everything out," I said. "But I want to keep seeing you."

Todd wasn't happy I wouldn't commit, but agreed he'd rather date me casually than not at all. I went to his family's house and ended up having an amazing time. He had the sweetest dog, and I hit it off with his parents, talking to his dad about his veterinary practice and helping his mom cook dinner. His brother, Daniel, is rather antisocial, but I even managed to get him to smile by the end of the night.

After dinner Todd and I hung out in his room, talking. I mentioned I'd recently been doing a little modeling for a small agency in Oklahoma.

"Really?" he said. "So are there pictures of you online?"

"Uh, I don't think so. . . ." I suddenly wished I'd never mentioned it.

"Yeah, right," he said, grinning. "I bet there are some hot incriminating photos of you in underwear or something. I'm gonna Google you."

"NO!" I said, definitely too loudly.

"Why?"

My heart was racing. "Just. Don't. Please don't Google me."

"But why?" He looked really confused.

"I don't know. . . . It's . . . embarrassing. Just don't do it, okay?"

"Uh, okay," he said.

"Please?" I said. "Promise?"

"Okay, yeah, I promise."

But I could tell I had only made him more curious. *Is there any way to get around this? Probably not.* I decided I should just accept that he was probably going to Google me and that he would discover I was transgender. I'd have to deal with the consequences, whatever they were.

"So did you have fun tonight?" he asked tenderly.

"Maybe," I joked.

"*Maybe?* You better have more to say than that!" he said and threw himself on top of me.

We wrestled around, laughing, and then he lifted my T-shirt and delivered a loud raspberry to my stomach.

I knew I had to definitively choose between Arin and Todd, but I just didn't know how. I loved Arin more than anything and couldn't bear to hurt him, and as bad as things had gotten, part of me still wondered if Arin and I could some-how, someday be happy together the way we once were. I was scared that if I broke up with Arin we'd never get that chance back. And yet, at the same time, I had all these new, exciting feelings for Todd. Rather than make a decision, I continued to date both of them. *I'll figure everything out soon,* I told myself. *Just not today.*

About a week after the night at his parents' house, Todd invited me for a picnic dinner in the woods. *What a sweet, romantic idea*, I thought.

But when the night came and Todd led me farther and farther into the dense forest, and the twilight sky turned from cerulean blue to pitch black, I started to get scared.

Oh my God. He Googled me, found out I'm trans, and now he's going to kill me. My panic may seem dramatic and kind of funny in retrospect, but the truth is that no matter how far transgenders have come, how much awareness and acceptance has come about in just the past couple of years, we still exist day to day as one of the groups at highest risk for being murdered. And no matter how much we may think we know another person or how much we may trust them, people are ultimately unpredictable. I had a Swiss Army knife in my pocket, and I clutched it. *I'm ready. I'm ready to do this if I have to*, I thought.

"This looks like a nice spot," said Todd, stopping by a bench. He sat down with our picnic basket and beckoned for me to sit next to him. It was cold, and I could hear the trees rustling in the night wind, the caws of strange birds. I sat down, hand still tight around my knife. I could feel my heart thumping.

"I looked up your name," Todd said. "And I don't care."

My heart was still beating wildly.

"In fact," he said, "I like you even more. Reading about

you and Arin, what you guys have been through, I realized how amazing you are. You're genuine, you're who you are, and I really, really respect you." His face turned to a shy smile. "I feel like I have to go save a bus full of children to compare to how awesome you are. And also, you're still the most beautiful girl I've ever seen."

I couldn't hide it—I had an enormous, goofy smile on my face. Todd took my hands.

"I know this is really soon. I've never done this so fast, but I think you're mature and I'm mature, and . . . I think I'm in love with you."

After years of wanting nothing more than the love of a hot guy, I now had the affections of two of them. And it was a nightmare.

As I've noted before, Arin understood me like no one else could. And the Arin I'd first started dating was perfect—he was romantic, sensitive, and the furthest thing from an asshole. He was the kind of guy who would always leave little romantic notes around for me to find. I would spend the night at his house and walk out to my car in the morning to see that he'd fogged up the window and written "I love you." In the early days, we could spend hours just lying in bed, staring adoringly at each other. I could bathe in the way he looked at me.

But our relationship had changed. I still loved Arin—I knew I would always love him—but dating him was making me miserable. It felt like we only ever did what he wanted to do. When I would make a suggestion, he'd just shrug it off. We fought constantly, bickering over the stupidest, littlest things. And there was the sex. Arin and I hadn't been inti-mate for a very long time.

With Todd, I was experiencing things—emotional and physical—I'd been curious about for so long. Whenever I saw Todd, I'd get butterflies in my stomach. We could laugh endlessly together, and he treated me very well. Todd and I always did things that we *both* wanted to do. If one of us didn't feel like doing something, we would find a compro-mise. I still loved Arin, but at this point, I had to admit I was in love with Todd, too.

I'm not delusional, though. From what I can tell, all rela-tionships eventually lose their spark. People get comfortable and they start to treat you differently. I don't want it to be true, but I'm a practical person, and there's no reason to think it won't happen with Todd and me.

I was also scared that if I broke up with Arin, it would mean losing each other as friends. Being there for each other emotionally—especially in regard to being trans—was a huge part of our relationship. When either one of us was feeling dysphoric, we could call the other up and know there was someone on the other end of the line who understood exactly what we were feeling. I may have had surgery, but I still expe-rience dysphoria—I just focus on other parts of my body. *My nose is too big, my shoulders are too broad, I wish my boobs were bigger.* Arin gets how that feels, and I get him, and there's no replacement for that. I was terrified that breaking up with Arin would mean losing that connection forever.

Every night I lay awake, desperately trying to decide what to do. Deep down, I knew I should break up with Arin, but as soon as I'd imagine doing it, I'd picture his crumpling face, his tears, how destroyed he would feel, and then I'd start crying. I hated myself for what I knew I was doing to him and Todd by lying. It wasn't who I wanted to be. I felt foreign to myself.

It's funny. I could summon up these great amounts of courage in terrifying situations. I could stand up against an entire high school of bullies and speak in front of hundreds of people. I was brave enough to be out and proud and put myself at potential risk in order to help others. But when it came to Arin, I couldn't find the courage I needed to do what I knew was right.

In the fall of 2013 I began my sophomore year of college, and Arin and I were invited to be guests on the *Trisha Goddard* show, a daytime talk show. We pretended to still be happy together. That was what everyone wanted, right? To express how I really felt would be letting so many people down, not only our moms (who were still our relationship's biggest fans) but also the public who looked up to us. It wasn't supposed to be our relationship that was inspirational, it was supposed to be our life stories—but I knew our romance made others happy. All I wanted to do was keep everyone happy, Arin especially.

In many ways appearing on *Trisha* was great. I wore a long blue dress with a batik print, a dress that used to belong to Arin—a detail the audience went wild for. We were on for a good half hour and were able to talk about things that were important to us. When Trisha asked if there was one message I wanted to get across, I said, "Yes. Listen to your children. You may think they're just young and don't know what they want, but you have to listen to them." It felt powerful and important to say this to such a large viewership.

But, of course, there were also the inevitable sex questions.

"Can I ask in general terms . . . ," Trisha said with an awkward smile, and I knew what was coming, even though I had specifically requested before we went on that the question not be asked. "Are you intimate with each other?"

The audience laughed.

Okay, Katie, I told myself. *You're charismatic. Just say something.*

"Pause for dramatic effect," I said.

More laughter.

Arin's only seventeen and still in high school, I thought. *How is this remotely an appropriate question to ask?* I wish I could have said something to that effect right then and there, but when you're in the moment, you panic, you go with the flow.

"Yeah, that's a curious question, because people want to know . . . ," I said.

Trisha turned to Arin. "You haven't had the whole operation yourself, have you?"

"No," Arin said.

"So does that . . . leave out a love life? Can I put it that way?" asked Trisha.

Trisha certainly had a narrow view of what could constitute "a love life."

"It's . . . not really there," I said.

"But it was never about that with us," said Arin, swinging his arm around my shoulder. "It's about the connection and the love that we have."

The audience applauded.

"We're just so *young* right now," I said—with pointed emphasis on the word "young"—"and just having fun spending time with each other and getting to know where we're at in life."

"Of course," Trisha said, smiling broadly as the audience continued to clap.

After the taping, Arin and I went out to explore New York City. I'd never been to New York before and was so excited to be there. I wanted to see Times Square, the Empire State Building, and Ground Zero, and just walk around and admire all the shops and people. Arin and I were on Broadway, debating whether or not to check out Bloomingdale's, when I got a text from Todd.

Hey, how are you?

Todd had been texting me nonstop ever since I'd left for New York, and honestly, it was stressing me out. He was insistent we become this serious couple, no matter how many times I told him I wanted to keep things casual. He'd been bugging and bugging me to change my Facebook status to: "In a relationship with Todd" and I'd finally just agreed, to get him off my case. I added the privacy setting "hidden," though, so no one else could see it. I still really liked Todd and wanted to try dating him, but it was getting too intense too fast. Also, he wanted to have sex all the time, and while I had really enjoyed it that first time, I wasn't so sure anymore. I'd recently been thinking that I needed to tell Todd that we should cool things down.

We should talk when I get back . . . , I texted.

Oh no. Am I in trouble?! he texted.

"Who are you texting?" asked Arin.

"No one," I said.

"Sorry. It's just . . . I want to enjoy New York with you," he said. Arin took my hands and tried to kiss me, but I backed away. I didn't feel like making out. I just wanted to explore New York!

"Let's go into Bloomie's," I said. "I want to see if it's really like in *Sex and the City*."

"Okay," said Arin with a pouty look on his face, which really annoyed me. It felt like the only thing he cared about was us walking around, hand in hand, him showing off his girlfriend. I loved him and knew that I would always love him, but all the stress and pressure was causing me to not even feel close to him as a friend anymore. Our whole relationship felt more like a business proposition, like Katniss and Peeta in *The Hunger Games*. I was only going through the motions for everyone else. I felt frustrated and trapped every way I turned.

That night we all ate Italian food at Carmine's, and I was able to have fun and relax a little. After dinner Arin asked if I wanted to come watch TV in his hotel room.

"Sure," I said.

We lay down on his bed, and he flipped on the TV. I was so exhausted from the day that I soon fell asleep on his shoulder.

"Katie! Katie!" a voice said in a harsh whisper.

I opened my eyes. Arin was shaking me, waking me up.

"What?" I said, groggy and out of it.

Denise was asleep in the bed across from us.

"I need to talk to you outside," he said. His face was pale.

Oh shit, I thought. *He knows I'm dating Todd.* I just knew it.

"Okay. . . ," I said, slowly getting up.

We went out into the bright, long, carpeted hallway. There were stacks of used room service dishes sitting outside various doors.

"Jamie just texted me. He said he went to Todd's Facebook page and saw that you guys are in a relationship. Are you dating *Todd*?" His expression twisted in pain.

I paused. I knew I should tell Arin the truth, but I couldn't. I just couldn't do it.

"No . . . ," I said.

"So then why is it on Facebook?"

"I don't know!" I said. I was digging my own grave, but as much as I told myself to *just tell the truth*, I only dug deeper and faster.

"Maybe Jamie got it wrong," I said. "Do we have to talk about this now? I'm so tired."

"I have a really bad feeling," said Arin. "I don't know what to believe."

"We're not happy," I said softly, averting my eyes.

"What?"

"You and I. We're not happy together. Why are we still doing this?"

"Because I love you! I thought we were going to try!"

"I'm sick of trying. I'm not happy, Arin! I think . . ." I hesitated for a moment. "I think we should break up."

Arin began to cry.

"You and I are *not* good together anymore!" I said.

"You never gave me a chance."

"I've given you a million chances! I've tried to break up like five times already!"

"Thanks. That makes me feel so much better." He looked down at his socked feet. "I really thought things were starting to get good again."

"Why would you think that?"

A man in a business suit came down the hall and put a key card in his hotel door. Arin and I were silent until he was gone.

"Us being here, on the *Trisha* show," said Arin. "The stuff we said on TV . . ."

"That's just what they want to hear," I said.

"So you didn't mean any of it?"

"No, of course I meant some of it . . . ," I said.

We continued talking in the hallway for hours, processing our relationship, everything good and everything that had gone wrong. Eventually we started to relax and were able to even joke a little.

"Remember on our first date at *Cabin in the Woods*, when I realized your mom and Wesley were there?" I said.

Arin started laughing. "Oh man. I was so uptight the whole movie!"

A look of sadness washed over his face.

"I don't want to lose you," he said.

My Arin. My sweet, funny, handsome Arin, who understood me like no one else.

"I don't want to lose you either," I said.

A grin spread over Arin's face. "So we're still together?"

"Yeah . . . ," I said. "I love you."

"I love you, too," he said.

As we walked back to our hotel room, I had a sinking feeling in my heart.

Arin and I returned to Oklahoma, and a few days later, our episode of the *Trisha* show aired. Along with the television broadcast, segments of the show also started popping up online. Almost all of the online segments focused on the sex. "Teen Transgender Couple Discuss Intimacy!" was the general title for every video. There was a three-minute clip of Arin saying he hadn't had bottom surgery and me saying we don't have sex. It felt like the message we were trying to get across was lost. As if all cisgender people cared about was, "Does your vagina work and does he have a penis?"

I understood that the media needed a hook, that Arin and I being a couple was something to spark people's interest and get them to pay attention. But it became only about us as some tabloid couple to follow. The fact that we each had an individual history, years of pain and struggle to become who we were, was shoved to the side.

One image of us that went viral showed us standing in our bathing suits with the caption: "DOES THIS COUPLE LOOK NORMAL? THAT'S BECAUSE THEY ARE." The intention of the caption may have been good, but what did it even mean by "normal"? That we passed as cisgender? Were heterosexual? White? Able-bodied? Attractive? If one of us hadn't been any of those things, would they still have called us normal?

Meanwhile, the deception of simultaneously dating Arin

and Todd continued to plague me, but as it turned out, the secret soon would no longer be mine to keep. About a week after we returned from New York, Todd contacted Arin.

I was getting dressed in the morning in my dorm room when I got a text from Todd.

I talked to Arin. We need to talk.

I was shocked. I was furious. I was *terrified*. But also . . . I was kind of relieved. At least it was finally all out there.

I met Todd by the library, and we sat down on the steps. His body was stiff and cold.

"So . . . what's going on?" I asked.

"I Facebook messaged Arin and then went over to his house and talked with him last night," he said.

The image of the two of them sitting in Arin's room, discussing me, made me feel like I might throw up, but I steeled myself. "Okay . . . ," I said.

"We know you've been lying to us. And we think you're full of shit," he said.

"You and I were not officially dating," I said. "I told you I wanted to keep things casual."

"You didn't tell me you were still dating Arin!"

"You kept pressuring me for us to be serious," I said. "I told you I still needed time. I *did* want to break things off with Arin, but it wasn't that easy. I tried like seven times. . . ."

Todd stared at me blankly, like he was still trying to compute everything that had happened. I felt terrible. I had put him in this situation. It wasn't his fault. Was I just a horrible person?

"You told me you loved me," he said. I had never seen Todd cry, but I could tell he was trying to force himself not to.

"I *do* love you," I said.

"Arin says you love him."

"I love both of you," I said. "But I don't want to be in a relationship with Arin."

My phone starting buzzing and I realized I was getting a flurry of texts from Arin. I took a deep breath and looked back up at Todd.

"I'm going to break up with Arin," I said.

"Does that mean you're my girlfriend?"

"It means I'm breaking up with Arin, and you and I can keep hanging out. I don't think I should be *anyone's* girlfriend right now."

Todd nodded, and I got up and left.

As I walked through campus back to my dorm, I called Arin. He was hysterical.

"I knew it! I knew you were lying! How could you do this to me?!" he cried.

"I'm sorry," I said, wiping at my own eyes with the back of my hand. Knowing that I was going to have to find the words to finally end things only made this conversation worse. "Why don't we meet up and talk?"

"Okay," said Arin, catching his breath. "I'll come pick you up."

Arin picked me up outside of my dorm, and we began driving around.

"I just don't get it," he said, starting to cry again. "I feel like I don't even know you." The car swerved as he turned to look at me.

"We should park somewhere to talk," I said.

"Where?"

"I don't know, somewhere quiet? Peaceful?" I pictured us parked on the edge of a serene cliff, staring out at a soothing nature scene as we talked. As it turned out, the only secluded spot we could find was a Taco Bueno parking lot. It would have to do.

Arin turned the car off and we sat in silence for a moment.

"Is it because Todd has a real penis?" he asked.

"No," I said in a firm voice.

"I can get bottom surgery," he said. His expression was desperate, almost wild. "I'll do it. I'll do it for you."

"Arin," I said, "this is not about that. You and I—"

"But you've had sex with Todd," he stated bluntly.

"Yes," I said.

Arin glared at me with what I can only describe as pure hate. "So that's all you care about? Having sex with a cis-male. After everything we've been through. You'd rather lie and cheat than—"

"This is not about sex!" I snapped. "I mean, yes, I was interested in being with a cisguy after my surgery, but—"

"I knew it."

I tried to gather my thoughts. "You and I haven't been happy for such a long time. And I'm *sorry* for cheating. I can't even tell you how sorry and guilty I feel."

Arin stared out the window at the few parked cars in the Taco Bueno lot. He took a shallow breath. "Is there anything I can do? Just tell me what to do. Please."

"We need to break up. For real this time," I said. It killed me to say it, but there was also a gush of relief. For once, I knew I was making the right decision.

"Fine," said Arin, his voice cold. "We're broken up. You

can date whoever you want." He turned and looked me in the eyes. "Just please do not date Todd."

"Arin . . . ," I stammered.

"If you date Todd, I will never talk to you again."

For a while, Arin and I didn't really talk. He held to his threat that if I was dating Todd, we couldn't be friends, so because I *was* dating Todd—though I still refused the label "girlfriend"—I avoided talking to Arin. I didn't want to hurt him anymore than I already had and I didn't want to get trapped in another cycle of lying.

Then, in October, Arin and I were asked to go to New York to be photographed by legendary photographer Bruce Weber for a Barneys New York campaign. We would be part of a series featuring all transgender models, and we'd get to see our photos blown up in Barneys windows, plastered on billboards across the city, and featured in fashion magazines such as *Vogue*. On top of that, we'd be paid for the shoot. When we each separately received the invitation, we were so excited that we, of course, had to talk immediately. As soon as we were on the phone, we sank into the familiar comfort of each other's voice.

"Can you believe it? Bruce Weber!" I said.

"I know!" said Arin. "And we get to go back to New York!"

I cringed a little at the memory of our last time in New York, when he had first found out about Todd. I could tell Arin was thinking the same thing.

"We're going to have an amazing time together," I said. "You and me."

Arin was silent on the other end of the phone.

"Yeah," he finally said. "We are."

A couple of weeks later, I headed to the airport with Arin, Denise, and Denise's sister, Susan. As Arin and I walked through the gate and onto the plane bound for New York, a flight attendant looked at us and said, "Well, hi, Katie and Arin! It's so nice to have you onboard!"

Arin and I looked each other. *Did that just happen?* I glanced down to make sure I wasn't wearing a nametag or something.

"You know who we are?" Arin asked the steward.

"Are you kidding?" he said. "I know exactly who you are. Your interview on the *Trisha* show was really inspiring."

We were sitting in coach toward the back of the plane, and the steward ended up spending much of the flight chatting with us, slipping us free chips and candy.

"I've stewarded Madonna," he said, "but you guys are even better."

As I looked out the window at the bright blue sky, munching my M&Ms, I had a startling realization. Back when I'd been a loser boy named Luke, I had created a fake twin sister named Katie as my ideal person to be—a beautiful fashion model in New York. And now here I was, off to New York to be shot by one of the world's most famous photographers, a guy who had photographed stars such as Nicole Kidman and Leonardo DiCaprio. Never in a million years would I have thought that could be a reality. But here I was, in the flesh, having somehow, unbelievably, become her.

I thought modeling would be a breeze. You just try on clothes, and people take photos of you, right? Dead wrong. It was exhausting. We had to get up at six in the morning, dress, go to the studio, do hair and makeup for two hours, get squeezed into complicated, impossibly tight outfits, go to Central Park, take pictures, put on different complicated, impossibly tight outfits, new hair and makeup, more pictures, get home at nine at night, wake up early the next morning, and do it all again. By the third day I was as sick as a dog and thinking, *Keep the money. I need to sleep!*

But it was also incredible. I'd always dreamed of being in an actual modeling studio with the white walls. It was a singular rush to know I was wearing tens of thousands of dollars' worth of clothes. And all the other models were *so* attractive. The first time I walked into the studio, I thought, *Oh my God, these trans people are beautiful.* It felt good to be part of a campaign promoting trans awareness. And it was especially fun to share the experience with Arin. Every time we were shot together, assistants who weren't familiar with our story would say, "You two have so much chemistry! It makes it seem almost believable!" *You think?*

The last night, Arin, Denise, Aunt Susan, and I went out to a nice dinner at a place called Landmarc. I was completely wiped out from the days' work and barely conscious. I ordered a lamb shank but couldn't even keep my eyes open to eat it. I lay my head on Arin's shoulder.

"Don't toy with that boy's heart," Aunt Susan said. "Don't you dare." And she started throwing little pieces of her bread roll at me.

After dinner we took the elevator down to the lobby of the Time Warner Center. There were two twelve-foot-tall bronze nude sculptures, one male and one female, facing the entrance. We noticed someone rubbing the bronze penis on the male.

"Everyone does it!" the guy said when he saw us staring. The woman with him took her turn. When they walked away, you could see that some of the bronze had rubbed off, making the statue's—remarkably tiny—penis stand out a shiny gold from the rest of the huge dark sculpture.

When in Rome, Arin and I thought, shrugging at each other. We went up and rubbed the good-luck penis too.

When we got back to the hotel, Arin gave me a hug good night.

"This has been really fun," he said. "I feel like we're getting along so much better."

"Me too," I said.

"So you still think there's a chance for us?" he asked with eyebrows raised.

"Arin, we're broken up," I said.

"Yeah, but maybe one day?"

"Who knows what will happen in the future," I said. "But for now this trip has been awesome."

"Yeah," said Arin with a sheepish grin. "I love you."

"I love you, too."

Then I went into my hotel room and passed out.

About a month later, around Thanksgiving, Arin and I finally got our chance to come clean to the world at large. *Inside Edition* contacted us about doing a follow-up segment, and we informed the producers that we had broken up. Both of us were a little scared, knowing this could mean the end of our media whirlwind. But frankly, it was time. Now there could finally be closure. *Inside Edition* decided to roll with it and film a special "breakup" segment.

The whole film shoot was pretty ridiculous. First they sat us down and asked a series of probing questions that had nothing to do with our being transgender advocates but was just relationship gossip.

"So who was the one who called it off?" the interviewer asked.

"I broke up with him," I said. "I just wasn't happy with the relationship. And I could see it was taking a toll on him. A toll on us."

"I was devastated," said Arin.

They kept probing, searching for the weakest, most vulnerable spots.

"Do you think you'll ever get back together?" the interviewer asked.

"We have a special, unique bond that no one will ever be able to fill," Arin said. "Nothing can ever break that, whether that be us as friends or us married one day."

Next they took us outside and filmed us holding hands, walking along a road scattered with yellow and orange fall leaves. They instructed us to drop hands and drift apart.

"Katie, what's your ideal guy like? Are you dating anyone new?" the interviewer asked.

I could not believe he asked me that in front of Arin.

"I'm just focusing on school," I said, blowing the interviewer off.

Then they had Arin call up his cousins who live nearby, and they had us all pose at a coffee shop. Arin's cousin Dewayne was supposedly my "boyfriend," and Arin's cousins Cheyenne and Amanda were his hot "girlfriends." It was supposed to represent us moving on and dating other people. Honestly, it was just plain stupid.

The segment titled "America's First Teenage Transgender Couple Split" aired a couple of weeks later. Arin and I were "officially" broken up.

I'm not sure whether I'll stay with Todd, or maybe one day get back with Arin, but I do know one thing. At the end of the day, I'm like my mom: I don't need no man. I can be just fine on my own. And truthfully, I don't even know what those boys are thinking—were they not listening when I told them about the Geurin Curse?

You're probably not surprised that a lot of my story deals with boys and dating—I am a teenager, after all. And sure, there's lots of drama surrounding my dad and little brother (though those relationships keep getting better). But there is one relationship that means more to me than anything else. The relationship that changed more than any other because of my transition was my relationship with my mom. Before I transitioned, it was always really awkward between us. I felt like we had nothing to talk about, nothing in common. We never bonded over anything. If you had asked me about her back then, I would have said, "Oh, my mom's a bitch. She doesn't care about me. She doesn't like me. No one likes me." It was me against the world.

The night I came out to her was the first bonding experience we ever had. It was the first time I looked at her and thought she was on my side. She didn't quite know how to handle it, but she was willing to try. As confused and scared as she was, she let me try on her clothes and told me it would be okay. It gave us something to talk about, something to interact with, and allowed us to build a relationship where today we're truly mother and daughter. I love her, I respect her, and I seek her advice and want to know her input in all areas of my life. I care what she thinks. And I know that I wouldn't be here without her.

The only sadness is that it had to happen so late. All mothers want to experience raising a happy child, but we've been able to do that only at the very end of my childhood. And now I'm becoming an adult. But I know we're both thankful for the time we've had these past four years. We've made up for a lot of lost time.

As for my relationship with God, I have moved from God-fearing Christian, to atheist, to agnostic, to now classifying myself as omnist or Unitarian. I believe that every religion is true and false at the same time. I don't know how the universe was created, I don't know if any being or collection of beings or energy is watching us, and I don't know what lies in store for us after we die. What I do believe is that there is *something* beyond. There is something that extends our existence after we die, and there is something that protects and guides us through life. Something made me cry that day when I looked up at the cloud in the shape of an eye, something that I *know* was not the cloud itself. Even in my darkest moments I have always felt that I had something pushing me forward. I have no clue what that thing is, nor do I really care. The only thing that matters is not to waste it. And to govern myself through what I think is right and what I believe my next course of action should be.

BEAR PEAK

It has been a year since Arin and I went skiing in Colorado. I remember it was over Saint Patrick's Day weekend, and Arin and I just couldn't stop fighting. But now it's Saint Patrick's Day again, and Arin and I are back in Colorado—this time as best friends.

On the long drive up we gave each other sheepish smiles, joked, and even slept on each other when we got tired. Arin had wanted to spend spring break with me in his favorite state. When he first suggested we go together, I was afraid returning to Colorado would bring back all the awful memories from that miserable trip and would negatively affect our current good relationship—but I was willing to risk it for Arin. As long as we stayed away from actual skiing, I was pretty sure we could have a great time.

"We'll just hang out together, enjoy the nice weather, and maybe explore the mountains!" Arin had said. I agreed.

Our group was large—Arin; Arin's friend Austin; Denise; Arin's cousin Amanda; Arin's little brother, Wesley; Denise's boyfriend, Nicholas; and Nicholas's son, Samuel. When we arrived in Colorado, we were all exhausted. We quickly got something to eat and fell asleep early. It was a good thing we did, too, because we were going to need all the rest we could get for the upcoming day.

Arin woke Austin and me up at the crack of dawn. "Hurry, guys! Get ready! We need to go downstairs and eat breakfast, and then the three of us are going to go climb the tallest nearby mountain!"

"Arin . . . it's seven in the morning, and we drove all of yesterday," said Austin, rubbing sleep from his eyes. "Everyone else is exploring downtown Denver today."

"Mhmmmmph," I groaned, and shoved my face into a pillow.

"I don't care! It's been my dream to climb a mountain, and I want to do it with you two!" Arin said as he laced up his hiking boots.

Austin and I quickly realized that we weren't going to be able to resist Arin's wishes—I could see in his eyes that he was determined to climb that mountain, and I could tell that he wanted more than anything for me to come with him.

Arin, Austin, and I made our way to the starting trail that lead to the summit of Bear Peak. We could see the famous devil's thumb visible in the distance. I knew the climb would be fun, and I also knew I was going to be very sore and tired the next day. But that was a part of it.

The climb was amazing. It took nearly six hours— between the three of us we had to take quite a few breaks to accommodate each of our needs and stamina. We laughed and joked all the way, poking fun at one another as we slipped on the snow and ice. I loved it. I loved the fact that I was climbing with friends—especially Arin. I had been so afraid when we broke up that our friendship would be lost forever. However, here we were, less than a year since our official breakup, stronger than ever. As we climbed, whenever either one of us needed a boost—a hand to help manage the more difficult ledges, a soft rub on the back, or a thoughtful look that said, *Keep going*—we were there for each other. Arin chuckled and giddily hopped when we got near the summit, in anticipation of reaching the top.

By the time we reached the summit, I was nearly spent. My lungs hurt, and my legs were shaking. Being afraid of heights didn't help either. However, regardless of my fear and nervousness, the view and the feeling that followed were incredible. Snowcapped mountains and hills shadowed by enormous clouds filled my vision. Below us sprawled the city of Denver. Skyscrapers and the few windmills that surrounded the mountain looked so tiny from up here. The chilly wind blew, hard and fast, but that didn't stop Arin, who was climbing the last few meters to the tip of the summit. Austin and I rested at the summit post, taking a few short breaths and snapping pictures before joining Arin.

"Arin! Don't you dare stand up! It's windy, and you'll fall!" I shouted over the forceful gusts. My heart pounded as I tried my best not to look down at the sheer drop. One wrong step, and I would plummet a few hundred feet onto jagged rocks, or possibly roll entirely off the mountain.

"Okay. . . . Okay. . . . Okaaay," I said to myself with ragged breaths. "Okay. . . . Don't look down." I sighed and closed my eyes. "Shit, I looked down. . . . Okay."

Arin was beaming, with a smile from ear to ear.

"I'll take a picture of us!" he cheered as he held his iPhone out to take a selfie with me.

Here we were, together, after all we'd been through. After our falling-out and after all the hard things that had been said, Arin and I still cared deeply for each other. In that moment I knew that no matter what happened between us, I'd always love and be there for him.

I could tell he felt the same. As Arin and I sat there, leaning against each other's shoulders, Austin just a few steps beneath us, the three of us taking in the scene, I realized just how symbolic this mountain climb was. I'm still young, and I'm still learning, but I've lived a very complicated and interesting life. When I was younger, I thought my life was worthless and that I didn't belong anywhere. I thought I had no purpose and that I was cursed. When I look at my life now, I see that it has been beautiful. My transition was like climbing a mountain. When we first began hiking Bear Peak, I was scared and worried that I might not be able to make it to the end. It took what seemed like ages to get to the top, all of us wondering when the sharp inclines would stop and the next flat resting area would come. But once I reached the summit and looked out at what I had accomplished, I knew that I would gladly do it all over again. My achievements and my story have made those important to me proud and, more important, have made me proud of myself. Through my journey, I have redefined "normal" not only to myself but also to my family, and hopefully to many others. Life is hard and scary—like climbing a mountain—but it's okay to be scared. What's important is to accept your insecurities and fears, learn to conquer them, and teach others to fight for what is right.

ACKNOWLEDGMENTS

I want to thank my mom for being the most influential person in my life. She has been there for me through every twist and turn in my journey—and she has been my guardian angel, my best friend, and my inspiration. There is no way I would have made it this far without her.

To my grandma, aunts, and uncles, thank you for your efforts to understand me. Although we aren't as close as I would like, I will always love all of you dearly.

Thank you to my therapists, Taylor and Brenda, for being patient and understanding of me and my situation.

Thank you, Tim, Ken, and all of the volunteers at Openarms Youth Project for making me feel wanted and included.

Thank you to all of my friends in Okay and Bixby, Oklahoma, who have loved and accepted me regardless of my identity—it means so much to me. Catherine, Maria, Lisa, and the large group of girls that I used to hang out with during my awkward years in Bixby—thank you from the bottom of my heart.

Needless to say, I must thank Arin and his amazing family. They have adopted me into their family and have made me feel as if I have a second home. Arin has always been there for me, and he has understood me better than anyone else. Arin and his wonderful, close family will always have a special place in my heart.

I especially want to thank those at the Tulsa Equality Center—Toby Jenkins and Laura Arrowsmith, specifically—who were there for me and my mother when no one else was. Those two amazing and lovely people held my hand through the hardest times of my transition. They taught me how to treat people and how to accept myself. Of course, I have to include everyone who dedicates their time and effort at the center, making it the amazing place that it is. I've never been anywhere else that was so full of love and acceptance, and I owe everything to the center.

Christian Trimmer, my editor; without his help this book would have never happened. He, along with everyone else at Simon & Schuster, has been wonderful. I hope that they will continue to help others and change lives like they have changed mine.

I also want to thank my friend and cowriter, Ariel. She has allowed me to continue with my education while being able to tell my story. She has become something like family, and I hope to always be close to her.

Thank you to Nancy McDonald, who was the mediator between my donor and me. She's an amazing woman who inspires me and who helped me through my transition.

Lastly, I want to thank the anonymous donor who paid for my surgery. I don't know who you are, and I may never find out. But I promise that I will continue to fight for equality for all, and to help those who need me. I will make you proud, and I will pay forward what you did for me.

TIPS FOR TALKING TO TRANSGENDER PEOPLE

One more thing before I go. I put together this guide for people who might need a little help understanding how to talk to or treat a transgender person. Gender and gender expression are very complicated and complex ideas. I've read a lot of books, trying to wrap my head around the concepts, and I still find them challenging. There are a bunch of different theories, and not everyone, including people within the transgender community, agrees on the particulars. So, just to be clear, I am not speaking for everyone in the community; rather, I am giving advice based on *my* personal experiences and ideals. With that caveat, here are some general tips that a large portion of transgender people appreciate.

I think everyone would agree that being called "it" or "freak" or the ambiguous "he-she" is offensive. These terms make people feel out of place and "othered." Those who are transgender may have lived their whole lives feeling like an "other," especially once they understood their true gender identity. **Tip #1** is to make transgender people feel understood, or at least make an attempt to understand. If you are sure that someone is transgender but are unsure of someone's preferred gender and gender pronouns (he, she, hir, etc.), then simply ask (only if you are in an environment that would allow such a personal question). Accept those who are transgender for who they really are and who they identify as. It is also important to **ALWAYS** keep confidentiality with a transgender person (**Tip #2**). Just because they are comfortable speaking to you, that doesn't mean that they are comfortable with everyone else. Most transgender people, even those who are out, do not like it when others find out about them through their friends or family. Let transgender people decide whom they wish to tell and when they want to tell them.

Personally, I enjoy it when people ask questions. I feel that it is my duty as an advocate to answer questions, even the rude and ignorant ones; I believe that is how we learn. When people ask what my old name is, I will usually answer the question. Or if they ask me when I "decided" to become a woman, I will first correct their wording and then answer the question. However, many transgender people do not feel the same way I do. Instead they prefer not to share details about their personal life and feel that the person they once were is no longer valid. They want to be seen, perceived, loved, and understood in the gender and form that they have worked hard to achieve—the way they were always meant to be. **Tip #3** is to respect people's privacy. You may not always get an answer to your questions, but please do not judge or degrade someone just because they do not want to share things about themselves. Make sure to respect the boundaries of your transgender friend. Ask them if they are comfortable talking about their past. Steer clear of asking them intimate questions. (They don't ask you what's in your pants, so don't ask them.) If they are open to talking, then— and only *then*—you can ask questions, preferably starting small and working your way up.

Tip #4 deals with sexuality. We're probably all guilty of assuming someone's gay or straight based on some random detail, like, "Wow, he's such a good athlete; he must be straight" or "Wow, she's such a good athlete; she must be a lesbian." But please do not assume that gender has anything to do with sexuality. The coming-out process can be really tough for LGBT people, and constantly being asked who of the opposite gender they're attracted to adds to the pressure to conform. Just because someone identifies as being transmasculine does not mean that he is attracted to women, or vice versa for a transfeminine person. Sexuality is fluid, meaning that a transmale can be attracted to men, women, all genders, or no one at all! The best way to think about sexuality and gender is this: sexuality is whom you want to sleep with, while gender is whom you want to sleep as. Again, my advice to you is to simply ask. Once you have your answer, you can have a more open, respectful conversation.

If there's anything you take away from this guide, I hope it's **Tip #5**, which is, it's okay to make mistakes. It is! You'll recall that I have been yelled at and attacked for misgendering people and for being ignorant! What I love most about people is that there could be ten people in a room, but with sixteen different opinions! It's all right if you slip up or accidently misgender someone—that's part of the learning process. However, what is important is to be open to learning. Be open to people correcting you (and be prepared for some to become hostile). Try your best to stay calm if someone does get aggressive. Simply explain that you are learning and that you don't mean to offend anyone. Follow up by asking *appropriate* questions and respecting each individual's boundaries. If we're going to make lasting changes, we need to have the uncomfortable, awkward, tough conversations.

People must understand that transgender people just want to be happy. That's it—there is no secret to it! Many transgender people lose their families and friends over their transitions. They are hated, beaten, abandoned, and even killed. But the worst part is that they often don't like themselves. Transgender people aren't out for attention or to trick people, to dress in the opposite gender's clothing and parade around. The entire purpose of transitioning is to be happy. It's about becoming the person who matches how you've always felt on the inside. Please do your part to support their happiness.

ILLUSTRATOR'S NOTE

The cover of *Rethinking Normal* is designed to portray Katie's experience growing up trans, but I hope that it also speaks more broadly to the nearly ubiquitous phenomenon of adolescent discontent and the parallel desire for a future of wholeness and authenticity.

The figures on the cover—a young boy casting a shadow of an adult woman—are meant to represent Katie's personal journey, which follows a fairly traditional, binary gender paradigm. This depiction is not representative of the trans experience as a whole, nor should it be. Personally, I identify as trans, and take testosterone, but I have no pronoun preference and have no desire to dictate how people experience me or my gender. I just want to be myself and hope that people will speak with and about me in a respectful manner.

I have a masters of fine arts in "Illustration as Visual Essay" and have been a professional illustrator for the past decade. I have done a number of other book covers and was pleasantly surprised when this one was offered to me, since the subject aligns so well with my personal experience and identity.

We went through several stages of sketches before I began creating the final art for the cover. I initially did a set of nine rough sketches. My focus was on highlighting Katie's strength. The line work is drawn in ink, and the color is a mix of scanned papers and scanned watercolor. The scanned papers are from my vast collection of ephemera: the grid paper is from a tailor's promotional booklet from the 1950s, and the envelope on the right came with instructional material for my first camera. The paper used for the upper portion is a blank page from a 1940s novel. While these papers were chosen for their aesthetic qualities, their previous lives are not irrelevant. The cover shows a child standing at the edge of grid paper (representing the rigidity of the gender system we are expected to go along with), literally given out by makers of gentlemen's attire, and the shadow figure, the hope of a future self, walks out into open space, under a blank page—the future to be created by the author, and the reader.

I've been making books ever since I was allowed to handle a stapler, and have gone on to explore many aspects of bookmaking, from binding books by hand, to publishing, to doing illustration work. My life could easily be chronicled by the book projects I've created or been a part of, and I'm pleased that this cover is now part of that history.

—*Lauren Simkin Berke*

RESOURCES

Throughout my story I've referenced books, shows, movies, and websites that helped me during my transition. Here's a list of a bunch of them, along with some others that are definitely worth checking out.

BOOKS

Picture Book

My Princess Boy by Cheryl Kilodavis, illustrated by Suzanne DeSimone, published by Aladdin, 2010 (A very special read for gender nonconforming children.)

Trans Young Adult Literature

I cannot tell you how much it helped me to see a version of my story reflected in these novels.

Luna by Julie Anne Peters, published by Little, Brown & Company, 2004

Parrotfish by Ellen Wittlinger, published by Simon & Schuster Books for Young Readers, 2007

Almost Perfect by Brian Katcher, published by Delacorte Press, 2009 (This one's great for allies.)

Jumpstart the World by Catherine Ryan Hyde, published by Alfred A. Knopf, 2010

I Am J by Cris Beam, published by Little, Brown & Company, 2011

Being Emily by Rachel Gold, published by Bella Books, 2012

Run, Clarissa, Run by Rachel Eliason, self-published, 2012

Beautiful Music for Ugly Children by Kirstin Cronn-Mills, published by Flux, 2012

A Circus Mirror Day by Corin Ash, published by Featherweight Press, 2012 (It's available for free download here: http ://www.featherweightpublishing.com/ShowBook.php ?HH=CA_CIRCUSMIRDAY)

Freakboy by Kristin Elizabeth Clark, published by Farrar, Straus and Giroux Books for Young Readers, 2013

Trans Young Adult Nonfiction

Beyond Magenta: Transgender Teens Speak Out by Susan Kuklin, published by Candlewick Press, 2014 (There's a really comprehensive resource guide at the end of the book.)

LGB Young Adult Literature

I read a lot of these books while I was transitioning. Though I didn't identify as lesbian, gay, or bisexual, I found some comfort in the similarities I had with the characters in the stories.

Annie on My Mind by Nancy Garden, published by Farrar, Straus and Giroux, 1982

Dare Truth or Promise by Paula Boock, published by Houghton Mifflin Company, 1997

Empress of the World by Sara Ryan, published by Viking, 2001

Kissing Kate by Lauren Myracle, published by Speak, 2003

Boy Meets Boy by David Levithan, published by Alfred A. Knopf, 2003

grl2grl: Short Fictions by Julie Anne Peters, published by Little, Brown & Company, 2007

Will Grayson, Will Grayson by John Green and David Levithan, published by Dutton Books, 2010

Trans Memoirs

I thank these women for sharing their stories.

She's Not There: A Life in Two Genders by Jennifer Finney Boylan, published by Broadway Paperbacks, 2003

A Queer and Pleasant Danger: The True Story of a Nice Jewish Boy Who Joins the Church of Scientology and Leaves Twelve Years Later to Become the Lovely Lady She Is Today by Kate Bornstein, published by Beacon Press, 2012

Redefining Realness: My Path to Womanhood, Identity, Love & So Much More by Janet Mock, published by Atria Books, 2014

Reads for Parents

These books were invaluable resources for many parents in my community attempting to learn more about transgenderism.

Transparent: Love, Family, and Living the T with Transgender Teenagers by Cris Beam, published by Harcourt, Inc., 2007

The Meaning of Matthew: My Son's Murder in Laramie, and a World Transformed by Judy Shepard, published by Hudson Street Press, 2009

Transitions of the Heart: Stories of Love, Struggle, and Acceptance by Mothers of Transgender and Gender Variant Children edited by Rachel Pepper, published by Cleis Press, Inc., 2012

Reads for Anyone Who Wants to Know More

I've read a few of these. Many of them were suggested to me by my transgender friends.

How Sex Changed: A History of Transsexuality in the United States by Joanne Meyerowitz, published by Harvard University Press, 2002

Gender Outlaw: On Men, Women, and the Rest of Us by Kate Bornstein, published by Routledge, 1994

Transgender History by Susan Stryker, published by Seal Press, 2008

Gender, Bullying, and Harassment: Strategies to End Sexism and Homophobia in Schools by Elizabeth J. Meyer with a foreword by Lyn Mikel Brown, published by Teachers College Press, 2009

Kicked Out edited by Sassafras Lowrey with a foreword by Judy Shepard, published by Homofactus Press, 2010

Captive Genders: Trans Embodiment and the Prison Industrial Complex edited by Eric A. Stanley and Nat Smith, published by AK Press, 2011

TELEVISION SHOWS

Dirty Sexy Money (2007–2009) was the first prime time show to have a recurring transgender character played by a transgender actress, the gorgeous Candis Cayne. She later showed up on *Nip/Tuck* (2003–2010) as the transgender character Alexis Stone. I was a little young to be watching either show, but I wouldn't miss the opportunity to see Candis.

Orange Is the New Black (2013–present)

Transparent (2014–present)

MOVIES

All of the Harry Potter films (They were very often the escape I needed growing up.)

Matilda

Ma Vie en Rose

WEBSITES

I can't recall specific websites that I visited to aid in my transition. However, with the current power and convenience of the Internet, it is as simple as typing "transgender" into a search bar and clicking enter to discover a world of information.

www.google.com—Google is your best friend.

www.youtube.com—YouTube is your second best friend.

www.okeq.org—The official site for the Dennis R. Neill Equality Center. The center was a haven for me. I'm incredibly lucky not only that it existed but also that it was close to where I lived. Hopefully, there's a similar center near you.

www.glaad.org/transgender—There's tons of awesome stuff on GLAAD's transgender page.

www.thetrevorproject.com—The Trevor Project provides crisis intervention and suicide prevention services to transgender, lesbian, gay, bisexual, and questioning young people.

www.glsen.org—The Gay, Lesbian & Straight Education Network works to make schools safe for all students.

www.pflag.org—PFLAG provides a lot of resources for parents, families, friends, and allies of the LGBT community. It has more than three hundred fifty chapters, hopefully one near you.

www.thetaskforce.org—The National Gay and Lesbian Task Force is all about full LGBT equality.

www.wpath.org—The World Professional Association for Transgender Health provided me with a ton of useful information.